D1454585

THE UNOFFICIAL FOOTBALL WORLD CHAMPIONSHIPS

AN ALTERNATIVE SOCCER HISTORY

PAUL BROWN

tonto sport

www.ufwc.co.uk

First published in 2006 by Tonto Press

ISBN 0-9552183-1-4
978-0-9552183-1-6

A catalogue record for this book is
available from the British Library

Cover and interior illustrations by
Robin Brown @ www.bornoffside.co.uk

The UFWC is not affiliated with FIFA, UEFA, the FA, or any
governing continental or national football body, nor any
individual club or player

www.ufwc.co.uk
info@ufwc.co.uk

Tonto Press
United Kingdom
www.tontopress.com

CONTENTS

INTRODUCTION

Welcome to the Unofficial Football World Championships – probably the least known but most exciting football competition on Earth.

This is how it works: the Unofficial Football World Championships (UFWC) pitches real international teams into a continuous series of boxing-style title matches. Winners of UFWC title matches become title-holders, and move up the rankings table.

UFWC lineage goes right back to the very first international football match in 1872, some 58 years before the first World Cup. Small wonder the UFWC makes a tongue-in-cheek claim to be the home of international football's *real* champions.

The idea of an unofficial championship was effectively born in April 1967, when 30,000 Scottish football fans travelled to Wembley to see their side defeat World Cup winners England in a famous 3-2 victory. The jubilant Tartan Army claimed that, in beating the official champs, Scotland had become unofficial champions. An epic trawl through reams of international football statistics more than justified their claims. Not only were Scotland at that moment the unofficial champions, they were also unofficially the greatest team the world had ever seen...

The story of the UFWC really begins with the first ever international match, played between Scotland and England in Glasgow on 30 November 1872. As Scotland and England were the only international teams in existence, the winner of this initial match could safely claim to be the best side in the world – the Unofficial Football World Champions, if you will. Unfortunately, neither side managed to win the match – the score was a rather disappointing 0-0.

So swiftly fast-forward to the second international football match, again between England and Scotland, and played in London on 8 March 1873. This time there were a full six goals – England won 4-2, and became the very first Unofficial Football World Champions. But they didn't hold the title for long. In 1874 they were beaten 2-1 by Scotland, meaning the UFWC title passed to the Scots.

The UFWC title bounced backward and forward between England and Scotland, and then Ireland and Wales got involved. The British home nations dominated the UFWC during international football's formative years, until the instigation of international tours and tournaments meant sides from all around the globe began to play each other. The first World Cup tournament took place in 1930 – and the then-reigning UFWC champs England were not invited to attend, making something of a mockery of the FIFA competition. The World Cup was won by hosts Uruguay, who became the first official world champions. But Uruguay had never played nor beaten England. So England remained unofficial champs – until they were beaten in the following year by Scotland.

Following the UFWC lineage through almost 800 friendly and competitive matches, we can trace how the title was passed between over 40 different nations during more than 130 years of international football. It has been held by most major European and South American teams, plus comparative footballing minnows like Australia, Israel, Ecuador, and the tiny Dutch Antilles. The title has been contested at World Cup finals and in seemingly meaningless friendlies. It has been won by the most celebrated players of all time, and by previously unknown and unsung heroes.

The UFWC also operates an all-time ranking system. Sides are awarded one ranking point for every title match victory. No points are awarded for a draw. As of 2006, Scotland top the rankings table, some way ahead of second-placed England. That is a source of debate, but in the early years the UFWC, like football in general, was dominated by sides from the British Isles, of whom Scotland won most title matches. Quite simply, you had to be in it to win it, and the Scots are top on merit.

The Unofficial Football World Championships remains very much, well, unofficial, but it has received a thumbs-up of sorts from FIFA. 'As long as people have fun with football and that it is played in the spirit of respect for all involved, the non-violation of the Laws of the Game and the ethics of sport, FIFA is more than happy!' exclaimed a statement from the FIFA Media Department. 'We wish UFWC fans a lot of fun!'

And fun is what it's all about. The UFWC isn't going to usurp FIFA or supplant the World Cup any time soon, but it does neatly fill the four-year void between the official tournaments, and there is a good amount of enjoyment to be had in watching an apparently meaningless international friendly match with the knowledge that the victor will become the latest title-holder in an illustrious lineage that stretches back 130-plus years. Every UFWC match is a cup final, and, for football fans, it doesn't get more exciting than that.

This 'official guide' to the UFWC is packed full of classic matches, key players, and amazing statistics. So pour a cold drink, plump up the cushions, and uncover an alternative foot-balling history – and a fresh perspective on the most beloved sport in the world. Game on.

CLASSIC MATCHES

Scotland and England serve up 'a splendid display of football in the really scientific sense of the word'

MATCH #1

Scotland 0-0 England
30 November 1872
Friendly

West of Scotland Cricket Ground, Glasgow

No Scorers

The Unofficial Football World Championships, and the glory that is international football, kicked off in 1872 with this very historic goalless draw – an undeniable anticlimax. Up until this point England had been the only international side in the world, which made arranging international fixtures slightly problematic. The English busied themselves by playing games against a 'London Scottish' side, but appetite for a real England versus Scotland clash was whetted by plucky Queen's Park FC's run to the FA Cup semi-finals in 1871. The cash-strapped Scottish club drew 0-0 with England's Wanderers in the semi, but could not afford to return for a replay. Wanderers were given a bye, and won the FA Cup. But Queen's Park's gumption so impressed the English FA that plans were made to send an England team north of the border to play an official Scotland side. The Scottish 11, selected by slightly impartial Queen's Park captain and goalkeeper Robert Gardner, consisted entirely of Queen's Park players. England selector and captain (and secretary of the English FA) CW Alcock chose an 11 containing players from nine different clubs. Unluckily, Alcock was injured in a league match in the run-up to the game and was forced to replace himself as skipper with star forward Cuthbert Ottaway. For the fashion conscious: Scotland wore dark blue shirts with lion crests, white knickerbockers, and red head cowls, while England wore white shirts bearing the three lions crest, white knickerbockers, and blue caps. Match reports suggest that England, playing with an adventurous-sounding 1-2-7 formation, produced an impressive display of attacking football. But Scotland, playing 2-2-6, defended resolutely. The *Bell's Life in London* journal described the game as, 'a splendid display of football in the really scientific sense of the word, and a most determined effort on the part of the representatives of the two nationalities to overcome each other.' At the final whistle, despite the lack of goals, both sides were afforded 'three hearty cheers.' Almost 4,000 spectators turned up for the game, with the gate receipts for the day totalling, fact fans, a whopping £109. But ultimately the first ever UFWC match produced no winner and generated no ranking points. Captains Gardner and Ottaway both left empty-handed. What a bally rotten show.

HALL OF FAME - CW ALCOCK

Charles William Alcock was a football pioneer, the instigator of international football, and – albeit inadvertently – the UFWC. As FA secretary in 1872 he noted, 'In order to further the interests of the Association in Scotland, it was decided that during the current season, a team should be sent to Glasgow to play a match v Scotland'. As an England footballer he missed the match through injury, but later played and scored in a UFWC match against Scotland in March 1875. Alcock, born in 1842, also created the first organised football competition, the FA Cup, with the first round of ties being played on 11 November 1871. The first FA Cup final was won by Wanderers – captained, naturally, by one CW Alcock.

ORIGINS OF THE UFWC

If the Unofficial Football World Championships' statistical roots can be traced back to 1872, the idea of an unofficial title was first born in 1967, and the foundation of the UFWC as an organisation began in 2002. In 1967 Scottish football fans claimed that, in beating World Cup holders England 3-2 at Wembley in 1967, Scotland had become unofficial world champions. In 2002, a caller to a football phone-in radio show echoed that claim, and threw down a tantalising statistical gauntlet. Who, the caller wondered, were the current holders of the unofficial title? Identifying the current unofficial champions required tracing the lineage of title matches from 1872 right up to date. Among the first to undertake this mammoth task was Pete Tomlin from Letchworth, Hertfordshire. 'It took an awful lot of work,' he said, 'but, as a self-confessed anorak, I thoroughly enjoyed it.' Other dedicated football stattos also reached for their record books, many encouraged by a query in Sean Ingle's The Knowledge column in *The Guardian*. Daniel Tunnard is an English teacher living in Argentina. He began the project while twiddling his thumbs during the school holidays. 'I thought it might be a bit of fun,' he said, 'but it did take ages.' Other keen statisticians came up with their own sets of results, and inevitably there were disagreements. Differing methods and rules meant that there were inconsistencies, omissions, ranking differences, errors, and alternative starting points. Stefan Georg from Bonn, Germany, used the 1930 World Cup finals as the starting point for his research, although the eventual outcome was the same. 'I think this is a great way of calculating the real world champions,' he said. With assistance from Daniel, Pete, and Stefan, the author sifted through the various stats and arguments, created the www.ufwc.co.uk website, wrote a feature article for *FourFourTwo* magazine, and put together a definitive set of rules and records for the Unofficial Football World Championships. The UFWC was 'officially' born.

MATCH #2

England 4-2 Scotland
8 March 1873
Friendly
Kennington Oval Cricket Ground, London
Scorers: Kenyon-Slaney (2), Bonsor, Chenery (England)
Renny-Tailyour, Gibb (Scotland)

Six months after the first UFWC match, a return fixture saw Scotland travel to London to face a new-look England side. A series of trials had apparently unearthed some hot new talent, and only three English players survived from the first match. Scotland also made changes, bringing in star league players Lord Arthur Kinnaird of FA Cup holders Wanderers, and Colonel Henry Waugh Renny-Tailyour of Royal Engineers (also a Scottish rugby international and England cricketer). Both sides had spent three months in preparation, and expectations were high. The match was played on a glorious day in front of a boisterous crowd of 3-4,000 spectators, including many travelling founder members of the Tartan Army. England grabbed the opening goal in the first minute of the match, when Captain William Kenyon-Slaney, an India-born Army Officer, scored from an Alexander Bonsor cross. Kenyon-Slaney was the first international and UFWC goalscorer – and he later became the first footballer-turned-MP. Under football's early rules the sides changed ends after this and each subsequent goal – and there was no half-time break. England doubled their lead after a slip by Scottish goalkeeper and captain Robert Gardner allowed Bonsor to score. But Scotland hit back. First a mazy dribble from Kinnaird set up Renny-Tailyour, then William Gibb bundled in an equaliser. But the Scottish team were tiring, and England took advantage. Kenyon-Slaney grabbed his second goal to restore England's lead, and Charles Chenery made it 4-2 with five minutes left to play. There was still time for the excited crowd to spill onto the pitch, but there were no more goals. 'Thus ended a match so pleasant and free from disputes that there was really no appeal to the umpires throughout,' reflected *The Scotsman*. English skipper and goalkeeper Alexander Morton, in his 40s on his international debut, would have been the first man ever to get his hands on the UFWC trophy, had such a trophy ever existed. Having beaten the only other international team in existence, the English could claim to be the best team in the world – the Unofficial Football World Champions. And the entertaining nature of the game gave the new-fangled distraction of international football a huge boost. 'If any proof were necessary,' wrote *Bell's Life*, 'there was sufficient evidence on this occasion to convince the most sceptical that football, if only aided by fine weather, is a game that could take its place among the leading pastimes of the day.' Goodbye shuffleboard, hello football.

HALL OF FAME - LORD KINNAIRD

Arthur Fitzgerald Kinnaird, the 11th Lord Kinnaird KT (Order of the Thistle), was perhaps football's first celebrity – a 19th century David Beckham if you will, albeit a Scottish one with a big red beard who played in knickerbockers, a jumper, and a cricket cap. Born in 1847, he played in nine FA Cup finals, won five, and scored in three. He played up front and in goal, when the fancy took him, and scored one of the very first recorded own-goals, in the FA Cup final of 1877. Lord Kinnaird was president of the English FA for 33 years until his death in 1923.

MATCH #3

Scotland 2-1 England
7 March 1874

Friendly

West of Scotland Cricket Ground, Glasgow

Scorers: Anderson, A McKinnon (Scotland),
Kingsford (England)

Well over 7,000 spectators packed into the West of Scotland Cricket Ground for this third UFWC match (ladies were admitted free, courtesy of the very gentlemanly Scottish FA) and many more fans watched from vantage points on surrounding buildings. Cuthbert Ottaway, who had missed the previous international, returned to captain a much-changed England side, with only forwards Charles Chenery and George Heron keeping their places. Among the England debutants was the rather magnificently-named defender Robert Andrew Muter MacIndoe Ogilvie, of Clapham Rovers. Skipper Ottaway told the press he had an even stronger team than last time. 'They were pretty confident of a victory,' reported *The Scotsman*, 'and their splendid condition when stripped gained them a host of admirers.' Scotland also reshuffled their side, with stars Lord Kinniard and Henry Renny-Tailyour missing out. Queen's Park's JJ Thomson, who had played in the previous two matches, was promoted to captain. Seven of the Scottish 11 played their club football at Queen's Park, and their familiarity with each other would have a major bearing on the game. The match overall was regarded as a fantastic spectacle that did much to secure the future of international matches. Reports remarked that the game should be remembered for its 'beautiful and scientific play'. England scored first through Robert Kingsford, but Scotland's Frederick

Anderson netted an equaliser just before the halfway point. Scotland's winning goal was described by *Bell's Life* as 'a scene which can never be forgotten as long as international matches are played'. The goal was scored by Angus MacKinnon, but created by the marvellous skills of midfielder 'Little' Harry McNiel, who was carried from the pitch on the shoulders of spectators after the final whistle. McNiel beat three English defenders with a 'dodging run', then played in MacKinnon. MacKinnon faked to shoot with his right foot, 'but in an instant the ball left the toe of the left and went clean through the English goal.' Scotland were victorious, and took the UFWC title for the first time. But *Bell's Life* heaped praise upon both sides. 'Although the game was won by Scotland it must be admitted that the English team played splendidly and, in an individual point of view, surpassed the Scotch team,' said the journal, 'but the latter, who all knew each other's play, acted magnificently together.' The Scottish team were able to display what *Bell's* rather neatly called, 'playing-together power.' It wouldn't be the last time that effective teamwork and a skilful midfield tormentor would see Scotland to victory over the Auld Enemy.

HALL OF FAME - HARRY McNIEL

Born in 1853, **Henry 'Harry' McNiel** scored six goals in 10 appearances for Scotland, netting five times in UFWC matches. At club level, in 1873 McNiel courted controversy by transferring from Third Lanark to Glasgow rivals Queen's Park FC. Sometimes incorrectly recorded as 'McNeil' or 'McNeill', Little Harry was a skilful winger – one of the very original creative midfield players – and one of seven footballing brothers.

MATCH #6

Scotland 4-0 Wales
25 March 1876
Friendly

West of Scotland Cricket Ground, Glasgow

Scorers: Ferguson, Lang, MacKinnon, McNiel (Scotland)

As Association Football grew in popularity, new teams began to join England and Scotland on the international scene. This first UFWC appearance for Wales was watched by 17,000 spectators – 10,000 more than had viewed Scotland's victory over England two years previously. It was also the first UFWC match to have a half-time break. Club football was already popular in Wales, and the Cambrian Football Association, quickly renamed the Football Association of Wales (FAW), had been formed just weeks earlier specifically to raise a team to face Scotland. The FAW is therefore the third oldest football association in the world. The FAW was principally formed by four Druids players – Llewelyn Kenrick, Dr Daniel Grey, and brothers David and George Thomson. Kenrick became the first secretary of the FAW, and the first captain of the Welsh international side. He set about placing notices in sporting papers with the aim of recruiting Welsh-born or Welsh-resident footballers. But Kenrick was criticised for ignoring players from South Wales. 10 of the 11 selected players were from North Wales, and just one from the South. Druids (now Newi Cefn Druids) supplied six players for the international team, Wrexham two, and Oswestry (now merged with Total Network Solutions) one, with the other two footballers coming from England's Oxford University and Wanderers teams. Kenrick, Grey, and the Thomson brothers all played. Interestingly, both sides boasted brothers among their ranks – Scotland lined up with star midfielder Harry McNiel on one wing and his brother Moses on the other. Moses McLay McNiel was also Rangers' first ever international footballer. The deadly William Muir 'Billy' MacKinnon was up front for Scotland, and Charles Campbell had taken over the captaincy from JJ Thomson. Unsurprisingly, the relatively experienced Scots dominated proceedings. 'The game was a very one-sided affair,' reported *The Scotsman*, 'and after 90 minutes of hard play the strangers had to succumb to the superior passing tactics – which, by the by, seemed to puzzle the Welshmen altogether – of the Scotch team.' Nevertheless, the newcomers managed to keep Scotland at bay for some 40 minutes before Vale of Leven's John Ferguson opened the scoring. However the second half was all Scotland, with James 'Reddie' Lang, Billy MacKinnon, and Harry McNiel scoring to complete a comprehensive victory. But perhaps the result was not as important as the occasion. Wales were established on the international football scene, and they would yet have their day in the UFWC sun.

HALL OF FAME - LLEWELYN KENRICK

Samuel Llewelyn Kenrick was the founder of the Football Association of Wales, and the captain and selector of the Welsh national team. Born in 1847, the tough fullback won five international caps and was renowned as a 'fearsome shoulder charger'. Shortly after hanging up his international boots he refereed the 1881 UFWC match between Wales and Scotland. There was no favouritism on display from the 'thoroughly straightforward' Kenrick – Wales lost 5-1.

MATCH #20

Ireland 0-5 Scotland
26 January 1884
British Home Championships
Ballynafeigh Park, Belfast
Scorers: Harrower (2), Gossland (2), Goudie (Scotland)

Although ostensibly a friendly match, this fixture was also the very first game of the very first British Home Championships (BHC), the world's oldest and longest-running official international football competition (later simply referred to as the Home Internationals, and running for 101 years until 1984). The competition was initiated as a way to formalise friendly internationals, and the arrival of Ireland on the international football scene meant there were four teams that could compete. The Irish Football Association formed in 1880, and the Irish international team, representing a united Ireland, played its first game in 1882 (they lost to England in a record 13-0 battering). But before the BHC could begin, the four football associations of England, Ireland, Scotland, and Wales had to address the small problem of the fact that each country played football under different rules. Prior to this, international matches had been played according to the rules of the host country. A meeting in 1882 saw the formation of the International Football Association Board to create and approve a uniform set of rules. Now the BHC could get underway. The format was simple – each side would play each other once, receiving two points for a win and one point for a draw. The winner would be the team that topped the league table after all six matches. This opening game was played at Belfast's Ulster Ground, Ballynafeigh Park, in front of just 2,000 fans, although *The Scotsman's* reporter remarked, 'the afternoon was one of the most boisterous ever experienced.' Ireland were skippered by Dr John Davison, while Scotland were led by the great full-back Walter Arnott. The match proved not to be much of a contest. William Harrower of Queen's Park and James Gossland of Rangers gave Scotland a 2-0 half-time lead. Abercorn's John Goudie hit a third in the second half, before Harrower and Gossland grabbed another goal each to complete the 5-0 rout. 'Arnott and [John] Forbes, as backs, defended in brilliant style,' reported the Scotsman. 'All the forwards played skilfully and well. Harrower and [JJ] Thomson made themselves especially noteworthy.' Goalscoring debutants Gossland and Goudie never played for their country again, while Harrower only made one further international appearance, despite scoring in each of his three matches. Scotland went on to beat England and Wales to win the inaugural BHC. For Ireland it was a painful initiation to the UFWC.

HALL OF FAME - WALTER ARNOTT

Scottish skipper **Walter Arnott** was one of the greatest defenders of his generation. A genuine sporting all-rounder, in addition to football he also excelled at cricket, tennis, bowls, and yachting. Born in 1863, the Queen's Park right-back played 14 times for his country in an international career that spanned more than 10 years. At club level, in 1884 Arnott won the Scottish Cup with Queen's Park – by default after opponents Vale of Leven failed to turn up. He subsequently won it in a more traditional manner in 1886 and 1890.

MATCH #55

England 9-0 Ireland
9 March 1895
British Home Championships
County Cricket Ground, Derby
Scorers: Torrans (own goal), Bloomer (2),
Becton (2), Bassett, Howell, Goodall (2)

This comprehensive goal rout was not England's biggest UFWC win, nor Ireland's biggest UFWC loss, but its extraordinary scoreline still deserves further examination. England had beaten Ireland 13-0 in a non-UFWC match three years earlier, in Belfast on 18 February 1882, so the result, and the emphatic manner in which it was achieved, should not have proved too much of a shock. England were captained by Preston North End defender Robert Holmes, in the last of his three appearances as skipper. Making his debut for England in his hometown was 21-year-old Derby County inside-right Steve Bloomer, lining up alongside another Derby forward, John Goodall. England played in familiar white jerseys, while Ireland played in very unfamiliar blue ones. Heavy rain failed to keep spectators away, with 10,000 fans packing into Derby's County Cricket Ground to watch their local goal heroes inspire England to victory. But they had some help from the Irish defence. Just three minutes into the game, perhaps struggling on a muddy pitch, Ireland defender Samuel Torrans put through his own goal. A minute later, Steve Bloomer grabbed a debut goal. Subsequently, Francis Becton, William Bassett, and Raby Howell (of Preston North End, West Bromwich Albion, and Sheffield United respectively) all added goals to give England a 5-0 lead at half-time. To Ireland's credit, they only lost the second half 4-0. First

Bloomer scored his second, next Becton did likewise, and then Goodall hit two. Both Bloomer and Goodall had scored braces in front of their home crowd, and at the final whistle England had won 9-0. It is hard to imagine that the spectators went home anything other than rain-soaked and completely satisfied. England went on to beat Wales 9-1 in Cardiff in 1896, with Bloomer netting an amazing five times – a feat only ever achieved by four England players (Bloomer, Howard Vaughton, Willy Hall, and Malcolm Macdonald). Bloomer missed the next game, and England lost the UFWC title match 2-1 to Scotland.

HALL OF FAME - STEVE BLOOMER

Stephen Bloomer wasn't content with being arguably the best footballer of his day – he was a star cricketer and baseball player too. Born in 1874, the tall, slim forward was known as 'Paleface' because of his apparently unhealthy complexion. He scored 19 goals in 10 consecutive games for England, and 28 goals in 23 matches overall. Having retired from playing, in an unfortunate case of bad timing, Bloomer took up a coaching position in Berlin just three weeks before the outbreak of the First World War. He was subsequently interned for three and a half years at Ruhleben, where he led his barrack to the camp football championship at the sprightly age of 43. 'Though his activities are now confined to the narrow limits of Ruhleben,' reported the Ruhleben camp magazine, 'Mr Bloomer's skill on the field of play has been a source of inspiration for our younger players and of genuine pleasure to the onlookers.' Bloomer returned to his hometown of Derby after the war, and died in 1938.

MATCH #67

England 13-2 Ireland
18 February 1897

British Home Championships

Roker Park, Sunderland

Scorers: Frank Forman, Fred Forman (2), Athersmith,

Smith (4), Bloomer (2), Settle (3) (England)

Campbell, McAllen (pen) (Ireland)

Another England versus Ireland UFWC match, another rout, and another brace of goals for the great Steve Bloomer. But Bloomer's feat was surpassed on the day by the goalscoring achievements of two of his teammates. England had taken the UFWC title from Scotland in their previous match, with Bloomer netting twice in a 3-1 win. The venue for this defence of the title was Roker Park, with 14,000 spectators turning up. Sunderland full-back Philip Bach was drafted in to play in front of his home crowd for his first and only England international. Those in attendance could have been forgiven for initially failing to realise how spectacular this match was going to be – a full quarter of an hour was played before the avalanche of goals began. Frank Forman, then of Sheffield United, got England's first, and his brother Fred, of Nottingham Forest, netted the second. It was Fred's debut, and the pair became the first professional footballer brothers to play for England (amateurs Arthur and Edward Bambridge played together for England in 1883, and scored in the same England match in 1884). William Athersmith of Aston Villa hit the third goal, before captain Gilbert Smith and star striker Bloomer both netted to make the score 5-0 at half-time. Fred Forman grabbed his second goal of the game in the second half, as did Bloomer. Skipper Smith, the old-school Corinthians forward, ended up with four goals, including three in four mad second-half minutes. Debutant James Settle of Bury also hit a second half hat-trick – he ended up scoring six goals in six games for England. James Campbell and Joseph McAllen, of Cliftonville and Linfield respectively, scored consolation goals for the sorry Irish. The fact that Irish goalkeeper James Lewis only had eight full fingers (he lost two fingertips in an accident) may have had some bearing on the final result, although Lewis did manage to limit the rout by saving a James Crabtree penalty. This was England's second biggest victory ever (after the 13-0 triumph over Ireland in 1882) and, taking into account goals for, the biggest ever win in UFWC history. It was the first of two UFWC games to be won by an 11-goal margin. 15 goals represents the most ever scored in a UFWC match, and 13 goals is the most ever scored by one team. Unsurprisingly, England went on to win the 1899 British Home Championships, beating Wales 4-0 and Scotland 2-1 along the way. The English then took the UFWC title into the 20th century.

HALL OF FAME - GILBERT SMITH

UFWC-winning Three Lions skipper **Gilbert Oswald Smith** was one of the greatest amateur footballers ever to play for England. Born in Croydon in 1872, he played centre-forward for Charterhouse School, Oxford University, Old Carthusians (a side formed for old boys of Charterhouse), and Corinthians, and scored 11 goals in 20 games for his country. Smith was also a first class cricketer – a high-scoring right-hand batsman for Oxford University and Surrey. He died in 1943 aged 71.

MATCH #73

Scotland 11-0 Ireland
23 February 1901
British Home Championships
Celtic Park, Glasgow
Scorers: McMahon (4), Russell,
John Campbell (Celtic) (2), Bob Hamilton (4)

Another hammering by another 11-goal margin for Ireland – this time without so much as a consolation goal. This was Scotland's biggest ever victory, and the biggest clean-sheet win in UFWC history. The match was remarkable for several other reasons, one of which was that the Scotland 11 featured two players called John Campbell – one from Rangers, and the other from Celtic. The Glasgow sides were already dominating Scottish football, and the national side overall contained five Rangers players and four from Celtic (Queens Park and Kilmarnock provided the other two). Among the Celtic contingent was Sandy 'Duke' McMahon, 'the prince of dribblers', and a prolific goalscorer. The moustachioed Duke McMahon was said to play football with 'arms held high, spread out like ostrich wings, head down, back slightly bent forward, enormous feet.' Despite (or perhaps on account of) his unique playing style, McMahon netted a first half hat-trick, with Hoops club mates Campbell and David Russell also scoring, to give Scotland a 5-0 half-time lead. There were 15,000 fans inside Celtic Park, and they must have been rubbing their eyes in disbelief. And Celtic fans would have been overjoyed when McMahon scored his fourth, and Scotland's sixth, just after half-time. There were plenty for Rangers fans to cheer as well. Scotland skipper Bob Hamilton was the darling of the 'Gers, and the Scottish league's top scorer in 1901. Not to be outdone by Celtic's McMahon, Hamilton also scored four goals – even quicker than McMahon had managed. Inside-forward Hamilton scored 15 goals in 11 appearances for his country, and topped the Scottish league's goalscorer chart six times. John Campbell of Celtic's second goal, squeezed into the middle of Hamilton's four, brought Scotland's remarkable tally to 11. For namesake fans, the referee was named Richard Gough, although as he was Welsh it seems unlikely he was any relation to the latter-day Scotland and Rangers hero of the same moniker. So Scotland retained the UFWC title in fine style. But for Ireland it was another crushing UFWC defeat. The Irish had now played 18 UFWC title matches, lost 17 of them, and drawn one, each time failing to take the title. But Ireland's time would come, perhaps sooner than this crippling result might have suggested.

HALL OF FAME - SANDY McMAHON

Alexander 'Sandy' McMahon was nicknamed 'Duke' after former French President Patrice MacMahon, Duc de Magenta. A bona fide intelligent footballer, McMahon was said to entertain friends with recitals of the works of William Shakespeare. McMahon scored six goals in six games for Scotland, and hit a massive 171 goals for Celtic during his club career. He was also the first ever Celtic player to be sent off in an Old Firm match, receiving his marching orders against Rangers in 1902. Born in 1870, McMahon's life was cut short by cancer in 1916.

MATCH #82

Ireland 2-0 Wales
28 March 1903
British Home Championships
Cliftonville Grounds, Belfast
Scorers: Goodall, Sheridan

For the previous 20 years Ireland had been the UFWC whipping boys. But things were about to change. This match was the penultimate in the 20th British Home Championships tournament, and Ireland sat just two points behind group leaders England. 'Neither Ireland nor Wales had full strength at Belfast,' reported the *Penny Illustrated* paper, 'and the football was not of such good class as one usually expects at international games.' But depleted teams were not the only factor – inclement weather would also have a major bearing on the game. High winds battered the players in the first half, sweeping the ball forward in Ireland's favour. The Irish were able to force a succession of corners, but failed to beat Wrexham keeper Robert Evans, and the half ended goalless. 'Wales had bright prospects of victory when the second half commenced,' said the *Penny Illustrated*, 'but the rain that fell almost immediately the players made their reappearance absolutely ruined the ground, which became of the consistency of dough. How the players kept going was a mystery, but they contrived to attain to a fairish standard, and when Goodall at last beat Evans with a very fine shot, the enthusiasm of the spectators found full vent despite the gloomy surroundings.' Defender Archie Goodall played alongside his brother John at Derby County, although the siblings played for different countries. (Archie was born in Ireland, John was born in England, and both were raised in Scotland. John starred for England in the UFWC in the 1890s.) Ireland scored a second in the final minute of the game following a goalmouth scramble. The goal was officially attributed to Everton forward J Sheridan, although the *Penny Illustrated* reporter credited MJ Connor of Brentford with the final touch. The game finished 2-0 to the home side, and Ireland took the UFWC title for the first time. They also moved to the top of the BHC tournament table, and, subsequent to a 2-1 victory for Scotland over England, found themselves level with those sides on points. The 1903 BHC ended in a three-way tie between England, Ireland, and Scotland. As for the UFWC, Ireland lost the title to England in their very next game.

HALL OF FAME - ARCHIE GOODALL

Archibald Lee Goodall was a world-renowned goalscoring half-back who played for Derby County, Preston North End, and Aston Villa. Tough and controversial, it was said that opponents were 'attracted as if by a magnet to the business end of Archie's shoulder'. Goodall almost missed the kick-off of the 1898 FA Cup Final for Derby because he was outside the ground touting his complimentary tickets. Born in 1864, he was 38 years old when he won the UFWC in 1903. After retiring from the game, Goodall toured Europe and the Americas with a bizarre vaudeville act billed in the programme thus: 'Archie Goodall (former greatest football player of the past decade) in his thriller: walking the hoop. Here is an indescribable sensation that has startled two continents. He will defy the laws of nature and walk the interior of a hoop 50 feet in circumference, five inches wide, three inches thick and weighs 200 pounds.'

MATCH #92

Wales 1-0 Scotland
4 March 1907
British Home Championships
The Racecourse, Wrexham
Scorer: Morris

Despite having made 34 attempts, by 1907 Wales were the only side from the British Isles never to have held the UFWC title. Not that Wales were completely unsuccessful at international football – they had beaten England, Ireland, and Scotland outside of UFWC competition. And the country now had a bona fide footballing superstar in Billy Merdith – 'the Welsh Wizard'. The former Black Park Colliery pony driver had only recently returned to the game, having served a three-year ban. Meredith was banned as a Manchester City player following a bribery scandal, but made a successful, if unlikely, comeback with Manchester United. Also among the Welsh stars was Arthur Grenville Morris, Nottingham Forest's all-time record goalscorer. Known as 'the Prince of Inside-Lefts', Morris was signed by Forest from Swindon Town for the then-massive sum of £200. When he wasn't banging in goals for club and country, Morris ran his own coal merchant business. The Welsh captain was legendary 6'1" 13 st. goalkeeper Mond Roose, who was transferred from Everton to Sunderland in 1907. A photograph of the Welsh team taken before the match shows them assembled in front of a packed stand in red shirts with laced collars, white shorts, and assorted makeshift boots. Pictured next to them is English referee James Mason – immaculate in a four-button suit, white shirt, and bow tie. The game itself was a tough affair played in foggy conditions, and it looked like finishing goalless. But, just a minute from the end, Wales' Grenville Morris pounced on a rebound and shot the ball into the back of the net from 20 yards. 'Great cheering naturally followed this unexpected success,' reported *The Scotsman*. 7,715 Welsh fans saw their side win the UFWC title for the first time without even knowing it. But there was to be some tangible reward for the Welsh. This game was another British Home Championships match, and the result helped Wales win the 1907 tournament, also for the first time. As for the UFWC, Wales initially retained the title in a 1-1 draw with England, but then lost out 2-1 to Scotland in 1908.

HALL OF FAME - MOND ROOSE

Born in 1877, **Leigh Richmond Roose** was an eccentric and imposing goalkeeper who won 24 caps for Wales, and played for, among others, Stoke City, Everton, and Sunderland. Regarded as the best goalkeeper of the Edwardian period, Mond Roose refused to play in gloves, and enjoyed waving to the crowd after making saves. He was extremely superstitious, favouring lucky garments, which, it was said, were rarely washed. The *Cricket and Football Field* paper once noted, 'His pants, we should say, carried about them the marks of many a thrilling contest.' As a keeper he was famed for a bravery bordering on recklessness, and for his incredibly long throw, which he put to use in later life as a renowned and decorated grenade thrower in the First World War. Roose was killed at the Somme in 1916 aged 38. His body was never recovered, and his name appears – misspelt – on the Thiepval Memorial to the Missing.

MATCH # 100

Hungary 2-4 England
29 May 1909
Friendly

Millenaris Sporttelep, Budapest

Scorers: Kesmarky, Grosz (Hungary),
Woodward (2), Bridgett, Fleming (England)

In this landmark 100th title match Hungary became the very first team from outside of the British home nations to take a bite at the UFWC cherry. For 37 years the title was passed exclusively between England, Ireland, Scotland, and Wales. England had already played European opposition outside of the UFWC, beating Hungary – and Austria and Bohemia – in the previous year. Now, having taken the title from Wales in March and successfully defended it against Scotland in April, England took the title into a short post-season continental tour. Hungary were one of the oldest continental international football teams, having played their first international match against Austria in 1902. They were also one of the earliest members of the recently-formed Fédération Internationale de Football Association (FIFA). They had won more games than they had lost, but those games had been against fellow fledgling footballing nations, and Hungary were no real match for the experienced English. Sunderland's George Bridgett scored the first goal in front of 10,000 spectators after just five minutes. Vivian Woodward of Spurs and Harold Fleming of Swindon Town added to the score to give England a 3-1 half-time lead. Skipper Woodward netted a fourth in the second half to achieve the 4-2 victory. Two days later the sides met for a rematch. England named the same 11, and raced to a 5-0 half-time lead. The

The final score was 8-2, with Woodward hitting four, Fleming grabbing two, and George Holley of Sunderland also netting twice. The match marked the final international appearance of Evelyn Lintott, the Bradford City right half, who was killed on the Somme in 1916. Indeed, the First World War also put a temporary stop to England's fixtures in Europe, and called a halt to international football and hence the UFWC. The day after beating Hungary 8-2, the same team – minus Lintott – beat Austria 8-1 in Vienna. But England would not play outside of the British Isles again until 1921, and the UFWC title continued to be passed between the British home nations.

HALL OF FAME - EVELYN LINTOTT

A teacher from Godalming, Surrey, **Evelyn Lintott** played for Woking, Plymouth Argyle, and Queens Park Rangers before signing for Bradford City for £1,000 in 1908. Born in 1883, right-half Lintott won four England caps, the last of which was the 1909 UFWC win. He was killed in action aged 33 at the Battle of the Somme on 1 July 1916. 'Lt. Lintott's end was particularly gallant,' reported a correspondent to the *Yorkshire Post*. 'Tragically, he was killed leading his platoon of the 15th West Yorkshire Regiment, The Leeds Pals, over the top. He led his men with great dash and when hit the first time declined to take the count. Instead, he drew his revolver and called for further effort. Again he was hit but struggled on but a third shot finally bowled him over.'

MATCH # 127

Northern Ireland 0-1 Scotland
3 March 1923
British Home Championships
Windsor Park, Belfast
Scorer: Wilson

Another UFWC win for Scotland, but this game is most notable for being the first in the UFWC record books to feature *Northern Ireland*. Prior to 1921, a united Ireland side played on the international stage. The Irish Football Association (IFA) had governed football across Ireland. But in 1921 Ireland was partitioned under the terms of the Government of Ireland Act 1920. Effectively, Ireland was spilt into Northern Ireland and Southern Ireland, or the Irish Free State (now the Republic of Ireland). Although based in Belfast in Northern Ireland, the IFA continued to claim to represent the whole of Ireland, continued to select players from the whole of Ireland, and continued to send out an international football team called, simply, 'Ireland'. This was despite the fact that a newly-formed body based in Dublin in the Irish Free State, the Football Association of Ireland (FAI), also claimed to represent the whole of Ireland, also selected players from the whole of Ireland, and also sent out an international football team called, simply, 'Ireland'. It was not until 1946 that the sides were officially renamed Northern Ireland and the Republic of Ireland. (Even then, both sides continued to select players from both countries until that practice was banned in 1950.) Officially, however, all results gained by the team known prior to 1921 as 'Ireland' now stand alongside results gained by the team known from 1921 as 'Northern Ireland'. Northern Ireland's first international football match had been outside of the UFWC in February 1921, also against Scotland, and also resulting in defeat. Two years later, Scotland were on their way to winning the 1923 British Home Championships. Ireland were not expected to provide much opposition, but actually the match was anything but a formality. 'On the run of the game Scotland scarcely deserved to win,' reported *The Scotsman*, 'for the Irishmen played very well indeed, and [William] Harper, the Scottish goalkeeper, had far more work to do than [George] Farquharson of Ireland.' Middlesbrough's Andrew Wilson scored the only goal of the game midway through the second half, netting a rebound after a Farquharson double-save. 'Wilson, who has been such a success in representative games in the past, did practically nothing beyond scoring the goal which won the match for his side,' said *The Scotsman*. 'Seldom has a centre-forward with such a reputation been held in such subjection.' Among the Ireland defenders held up for praise was former Newcastle United full-back Bill McCracken, who, at the veteran age of 39, had just retired from club football and been appointed manager of Hull City. It is perhaps little wonder that Andrew Wilson struggled against a defence marshalled by McCracken – during his time at Newcastle, McCracken was credited with inventing the offside trap. So the IFA's Ireland side lost their first UFWC match as Northern Ireland. But the side formerly known as Ireland did eventually win a UFWC match as Northern Ireland, in 1927, when they beat England 2-0.

MATCH # 155

England 5-2 Scotland
5 April 1930
British Home Championships
Wembley Stadium, London
Scorers: Watson (2), Rimmer (2), Jack (England)
Fleming (2) (Scotland)

58 years after the first international football match, FIFA finally got around to organising an official Championships. And the 1930 FIFA World Cup finals competition in Uruguay was something of a farce. FIFA formed in 1904, and began to organise amateur football competitions under the umbrella of the Olympic Games. Uruguay won footballing gold at the Olympics in 1924, and that country was duly selected to host the first independent world football tournament. But there were problems from the start. Europe was in economic turmoil, and many nations decided they could not afford to send teams on the long sea journey to South America. There was no qualifying competition, and the 13 participants were selected by invitation only. The Unofficial Football World Champions – then England, having beaten Scotland in this UFWC match – were not even invited by FIFA to participate. There was some suggestion that allowing the vastly experienced teams from the British Isles to compete would be unfair on fledgling football nations. So England, Ireland, Scotland, and Wales stuck to their own British Home Championships – arguably a more competitive competition at this time than the World Cup – and of course they continued to contest the UFWC. This title match was watched by a massive crowd of 87,375 spectators, 7,000 more than watched the World Cup final in Uruguay. England were led by the great

David Jack, who had recently become the first five-figure foot-baller after his £10,800 move from Bolton to Arsenal. Jack won nine England caps, four of them as skipper. Also among the England side were flying winger Ellis Rimmer and penalty-taking half-back Albert Strange, both of Sheffield Wednesday, plus West Ham's Vic Watson, who scored 41 league goals in the 1929/30 season – an enduring club record. The England team were trained by Arsenal back room assistant Thomas Whittaker, although he was responsible solely for the physical fitness of the side and could not be considered a coach or man-ager in the modern sense. Scotland's skipper was David Meik-lejohn, also captain of Rangers, and later to become the editor of the *Daily Record*. Also in the Scotland side were Rangers forwards James Fleming and Alan Lauder Morton. But in the end this was a very one-sided affair. England were 4-0 up at half-time, although the Scots can take some pride from the fact that they 'won' the second half 2-1. Watson and Rimmer both scored braces for England, and captain Jack got the other goal. James Fleming hit both consolation goals for Scotland. The result meant England retained the UFWC, and pipped Scotland to the 1929/30 BHC title. Over in South America, Uruguay won the World Cup tournament, and the Victoire aux Ailes d'Or trophy, to become the first official football world champions. But Uruguay had never played nor beaten England. So England remained Unofficial Football World Champions – until they were beaten in the following year by – surprise, surprise – Scotland.

MATCH # 161

Austria 5-0 Scotland
16 May 1931
Friendly

Hohe Warte, Vienna

Scorers: Zischek (2), Sindelar, Schall, Vogel (Austria)

Hungary, Belgium, Luxembourg, France, Norway, Germany, and the Netherlands had all tried and failed to release the British Isles' grip on the UFWC title. Austria had made two failed attempts, but were hoping to be third time lucky against current champions Scotland. The Scottish team, like all British sides, was selected by committee, with scant regard for coaching or management. The Austrian team was a somewhat different proposition. New Austrian coach Dr Hugo Meisl was a bona fide football pioneer, and perhaps the first great football manager. The son of a Jewish banker, Meisl abandoned a promising career in finance to travel around Europe learning everything he could about the game of football. Using his amassed great knowledge of the game, he became a successful club coach, and then began to shape the Austrian national side into his 'Wunderteam'. But Meisl didn't work alone. His head coach was an Englishman who had learnt everything he knew about football from Scottish professionals. Jimmy Hogan had been a distinctly average inside-right who was taught the fine points of football tactics by his Scottish teammates at Fulham. The Scots played a highly effective 'scientific' passing game that relied upon steady, patient play. Hogan was recruited by Meisl to teach the Austrians how to play in the same way. The style of play Hogan instilled in the Austrians became known as the Vienna School of Football. And what better way to test the

Wunderteam's passing game than against the country that had invented it? Scotland, captained by Clyde's Daniel Blair, arrived in Vienna without their contingent of Rangers and Celtic players. They were promptly battered. With Meisl and Hogan orchestrating matters from the sidelines, the Wunderteam passed the Scots to death. Karl Zischek scored two goals, the great Matthias Sindelar added a third, and Anton Schall and Adolf Vogel completed the turnover. The UFWC trophy left the British Isles for the very first time, as Austria became the first non-British side to win the UFWC title after 59 years of UFWC title matches. Scotland were beaten at their very own game.

HALL OF FAME - JIMMY HOGAN

Born in Nelson, Lancashire, in 1882, **James Hogan** played for Bolton, Burnley, Fulham, Rochdale, and Swindon, but didn't really make a name for himself until he turned his hand to coaching. Hogan helped coach the famous Austrian 'Wunderteam' in the 1930s, despite having been interned by the Austrians at the outbreak of the First World War. Something of a contradiction, the Englishman taught the Austrians the 'Scottish game', and in 1931 helped Austria take the UFWC title away from the British Isles at Scotland's expense. He later coached in Hungary, and laid the foundations for that country's 'Magnificent Maygars' side of the 1950s. Sometimes regarded as a traitor in his homeland for taking his football knowledge to the continent, Hogan died in Burnley in 1974 aged 91. Tributes called him a founding father of the modern game.

MATCH # 173

England 4-3 Austria
7 December 1932
Friendly
Stamford Bridge, London
Scorers: Hampson (2), Crooks, Houghton (England)
Zischek (2), Sindelar (Austria)

A century on from the original Battle of Stamford Bridge, the setting saw another legendary scuffle. England were still regarded as the best team in the world, but Dr Hugo Meisl and Jimmy Hogan's Austrian Wunderteam provided fearsome opposition. The Austrians had held the UFWC title for 12 consecutive games, impressively beating Hungary 8-2, Germany 5-0 and 6-0, and Switzerland 8-1 along the way. Add to the equation the fact that Austria played Meisl and Hogan's brand of 'Scottish football', and this was a mouthwatering and monumental clash. The illustrated souvenir programme produced for the match (price 3d) showed the flags of both countries and photographs of captains Billy Walker and Karl Rainer. 42,000 spectators crammed into the ground, and the game got underway at 2.15 in the afternoon. Despite Austria's impressive passing play, England prevailed in the first half, taking 2-0 lead into the interval courtesy of Samuel Crooks of Derby County and Blackpool's Jimmy Hampson. But, six minutes after the restart, Karl Zischek pulled a goal back for the Wunderteam. Now the game became a classic footballing contest, with both sides drawing admiration from all in attendance. In the 77th minute Aston Villa striker William Houghton scored a third goal for England. But Austria were not beaten yet. Three minutes later the brilliant Matthias Sindelar pulled another goal back for the

Wunderteam. England replied almost immediately, with Hampson grabbing his second goal of the match to make it 4-2. But still Austria would not lie down. With three minutes left to play Zischek, who scored twice against Scotland in 1930, claimed another brace to put Austria within touching distance of England at 4-3. But that would be as close as Austria would come. England held out for a narrow victory but, to use a well-worn cliché, football had been the big winner. The game would go down in history as one of the very finest ever played. Austrian goalscorers Mathias Sindelar and Karl Zischek went on to become football legends, but England's two-goal hero Jimmy Hampson never played for his country again and was largely forgotten. In 1938 he was lost at sea while fishing with friends. His yacht, Defender, collided with a trawler. His body was never recovered.

HALL OF FAME - MATTHIAS SINDELAR

Matthias Sindelar, 'The Paper Dancer' and 'The Mozart of Football', was the playmaker and goalscorer at the heart of the legendary Austrian Wunderteam of the 1930s. Skilful and creative, Sindelar scored 27 goals in 44 games for the national side. When Nazi Germany took control of Austria in 1938, Sindelar refused to play for the newly-formed combined Austria/Germany side. A year later he was found dead in mysterious circumstances, officially from carbon monoxide poisoning. Despite the pressures of war, 20,000 people turned out for his funeral. Sindelar is still regarded as Austria's greatest ever player, and was voted the greatest Austrian sportsman of the 20th century.

MATCH # 179

England 3-2 Italy
14 November 1934
Friendly

Highbury, London

Scorers: Brook (2), Drake (England)

Meazza (2) (Italy)

This was truly a clash of footballing titans. England were the unofficial champions, still widely regarded as the best team in the world, and Italy were the official champions, having won the World Cup five months earlier. Italy were coached by the great Vittorio Pozzo, and had lost only four out of 34 games under the tactical maestro. 'Il Vecchio Maestro' ('the Old Master') is credited with establishing the Italian *metodo* system of pragmatic defending and precise counter attacking. The Italians lined up with nine World Cup winners, including the great goalscorer Giuseppe 'Peppino' Meazza, and three controversial South American 'ringers', including Luis Monti, who uniquely played in the 1930 World Cup final for Argentina and in the 1934 World Cup final for Italy. ('If they can die for Italy, they can play football for Italy,' Pozzo reasoned.) England, still selected by committee, had never been beaten on home turf by continental opposition. They offered debuts to Arsenal duo George Male and Ted Drake. Indeed, seven members of the England team were Arsenal players, including Cliff Bastin, Frank Moss, and skipper Eddie Hapgood. Their Highbury home ground was rammed with more than 56,000 supporters, and enveloped in fog and rain. That the match is remembered as 'the Battle of Highbury' says much about what followed. Within a minute of the kick-off England won a penalty. But Manchester City striker

Eric Brook saw his spot-kick brilliantly saved by Italian keeper Carlo Ceresoli. 60 seconds later Ted Drake got stuck into a tackle with Luis Monti that saw the Italian stretchered from the field with a dislocated kneecap. The furious Italians, forced to play the remaining 88 minutes with 10 men, were convinced that the injury had been inflicted deliberately, and began to kick and lash out at the English. Undeterred, Brook immediately made up for his penalty miss by heading a third-minute goal. He added a second direct from a free-kick in the 10th minute, and Drake made it 3-0 in the 12th. But the Italians' kicking game was beginning to take its toll on the English. Hapgood had his nose broken, and was forced to leave the field for 15 minutes. Brook suffered a broken arm, and Drake acquired two black eyes and a cut leg, although both played on. Several other England players suffered bruises and cuts. At half-time, as England patched up their wounds, Italy calculated a come-back. Perhaps coach Pozzo reminded his charges that Mussolini, who had offered the team huge win bonuses, would not accept sporting failure. Certainly it was a more focussed and determined Italian side that emerged after the interval. As the game restarted in pouring rain, the brilliant Peppino Meazza took control of the game, scoring two goals in quick succession in the 58th and 62nd minutes, before hitting the crossbar, and forcing Frank Moss into a raft of saves. Ultimately, however, the battered English were able to hold out against the 10-man Italians. England won the battle between unofficial and official champions by the skin of their loosened teeth.

MATCH # 193

Netherlands 1-3 Scotland
21 May 1938
Friendly

Olympic Stadium, Amsterdam

Scorers: Vente (Netherlands),

Black, Murphy, Walker (Scotland)

Scotland had beaten England 1-0 at Wembley in April 1938 to regain the UFWC title. Tommy Walker scored the goal that defeated a brilliant England side, and his teammates that day included a young debutant named Bill Shankly. Shanks missed out on the trip to the Netherlands, although he would return to the Scotland side for subsequent matches. The Scotland side that travelled was skippered by George Brown of Rangers, and included four Hearts players, three from Rangers, two from Blackpool, one from Celtic, and one from Third Lanark. But Walker, of Hearts, was undoubtedly the star of the show. The 50,000-strong Dutch crowd roared their appreciation as the inside-right produced a series of mazy dribbles that dumbfounded the home defence. But the Netherlands also produced good attacking moves, which the Scottish defence battled hard to break up. One Dutch shot was blocked by George Brown's face. 'His nose bled a good deal,' reported *The Scotsman*, 'but after attention from his trainer he carried on.' Scotland's technical superiority began to show as the game wore on, but several missed opportunities meant that the score at half-time was 0-0. But Scotland found their shooting boots early in the second half. The Netherlands' defence were appealing for offside as Andrew Black of Hearts drove home a low right-footed shot. Dutch players and fans remonstrated loudly, but English referee

Charles Argent waved away their appeals. Five minutes later Scotland extended their lead, with Francis Murphy of Celtic bursting through from the left wing to find the net. The victory was sealed in the 69th minute, when Walker deservedly scored, heading the ball home from an Alex Munro corner kick. To their credit, the Netherlands never gave up, with inside-left Freek van der Veen creating several good chances. Four minutes from time Dutch centre-forward Leen Vente stabbed home a consolation goal. After the game, Scottish Football Association secretary George Graham commented with remarkable insight, 'It was a good match and the better team won.' Despite being unofficial champions, Scotland were not invited to participate in the 1938 World Cup finals, a tournament subsequently won by Italy. Scotland held off UFWC challenges from Northern Ireland, Wales, and Hungary, but lost out to England in 1939.

HALL OF FAME - TOMMY WALKER

Thomas Walker OBE was an outstanding goalscorer and a gentleman of football. Born in Livingston in 1915, inside-right Walker, the son of Scottish international forward Bobby, played most of his career for Hearts. He won the UFWC with his country in 1938, and would have shone at that year's World Cup tournament had Scotland been allowed to participate. Walker died in 1993, but will be remembered for his goals and a remarkable selflessness. 'Scoring was often the easiest part,' he remarked. 'As often as not, a teammate had done some wonderful work in getting the ball over to me. He was the one who deserved the praise.'

MATCH # 199

Yugoslavia 2-1 England
18 May 1939
Friendly

Beogradski SK Stadium, Belgrade

Scorers: Glisovic, Perlic (Yugoslavia),

Broome (England)

Spring of 1939, and dark clouds were forming over Europe, with the Nazi threat brooding, and the German army already occupying Czechoslovakia. Ironically, the Nazi occupation of Czechoslovakia followed Neville Chamberlain's 'Peace in our Time' deal with Adolf Hitler, which in turn followed a highly controversial 1938 friendly football match between Germany and England in Berlin. As the teams lined up for that game, the England players, under pressure from the British authorities, shamefully issued a Nazi salute. England subsequently won the match, but history would show that to be of little consolation. Yugoslavia had close links with England, and would become an important ally during the war. But this was all about football. Yugoslavia were anything but newcomers to the international game – this was their 100th international match – but they were still expected to be overrun by the famous England team. England had never lost a UFWC match to opposition from out-side the British Isles, and they boasted a formidable line-up. They were still trained by Thomas Whittaker, and their team sheet was a veritable who's who of pre-war football legends, including Eddie Hapgood, Stan Cullis, George Male, Joe Mercer, Stanley Matthews and Tommy Lawton. But if England's team looked strong on paper, Yugoslavia's proved stronger on grass. Frank Broome of Aston Villa netted for England, but it wasn't enough, with Svetislav Glisovic and Nikola Perlic scoring to give Yugoslavia a 2-1 win. Both Yugoslavian goalscorers played for Belgrade clubs – Glisovic for Beogradski SK, and Perlic for SK Jugoslavija. 35,000 fans saw them score for their country in their home city. Yugoslavia had pulled off a huge upset, defeating a side renowned across Europe as the best in the world. It was the first time England had lost a UFWC match to a team from outside of the British home nations. The legendary England team lost the title, and many of its stars were about to have their careers cut short by the war. Of the 11 players that took on Yugoslavia, only Tommy Lawton would retain his place in the post-war England side. Yugoslavia lost the UFWC title to Italy in their next game. Then, in September 1939, a little over three months after this match, Germany invaded Poland. The world would never be the same again.

HALL OF FAME - EDDIE HAPGOOD

Edris Albert 'Eddie' Hapgood made his England debut in 1933, and became captain in 1934, leading his side to five UFWC victories. Born in 1908, Hapgood was a milkman and part-time Kettering Town defender before Herbert Chapman signed him for Arsenal for £950 in 1927. He won five League Championships and two FA Cups with his club, and won 30 caps for his country, captaining England 21 times. Like so many of his contemporaries, Hapgood's playing career was cut short by the Second World War. Hapgood went on to manage Watford and Blackburn, and then left football to run YMCA hostels. He died in 1973.

MATCH # 221

Germany 2-3 Sweden
20 September 1942
Friendly

Olympiastadion, Berlin

Scorers: Lehner, Klingler (Germany)

Nyberg, Carlsson, Martensson (Sweden)

During the Second World War, the German side played scores of international matches against occupied and neutral countries. For Nazi Germany, football was an important propaganda tool, used to demonstrate Nazi superiority and boost citizens' morale. Led by coach Sepp Herberger – a fully paid-up member of the Nazi Party – the side appeared in the 1941 propaganda film *Das Grosse Spiel*, or *The Great Game*. Not featured in the film was former international goalscoring hero Julius Hirsch, a German Jew who was axed from the Nazi team and subsequently died in Auschwitz. In April 1941 Germany thrashed Hungary 7-0 in Cologne to take the title. But two weeks later, on Hitler's birthday, Germany lost 2-1 to Switzerland in Berne. The Nazi regime was furious, with Goebbels himself declaring that there would be in the future 'definitely no sporting exchanges when the result is the least bit unpredictable.' Herberger was ordered to have the side train heavily for three full weeks before every subsequent international. And the German players had an added incentive to win – if they played badly they would be dropped from the squad and sent to the Eastern Front, where they would face almost certain death. The Germans duly recaptured the UFWC title from Hungary in May 1942 before comfortably seeing off Bulgaria (3-0) and Romania (7-0). They were fully expected to brush Sweden aside in a similarly emphatic manner. Sweden travelled to Berlin without coach and FA executive Carl Linde, who stayed at home after making negative remarks about the Germans. Before kick-off, in front of 98,000 spectators in the Olympiastadion, the Swedish players lined up with their arms by their sides as the Germans offered Hitler salutes. Then, seven minutes into the match, Sweden had the audacity to take the lead through Nyberg. Of course the Germans were no pushovers, and they fought back to take a 2-1 lead through Ernst Lehner and August Klingler. But Sweden were level before half-time, with Carlsson grabbing an equaliser. And the second half belonged to the Swedes, with Martensson netting in the 71st minute to seal a brave victory. The defeat marked the beginning of the end for the Nazi Germany team. '100,000 have left the stadium depressed,' remarked foreign affairs secretary Martin Luther, 'and because victory in this football match is closer to these people's hearts than the capture of some city in the East, such an event must be prohibited for the sake of the domestic mood.' The final straw for the Nazi regime was a non-UFWC 5-2 defeat to Slovakia in November 1942. The national team was dissolved, and its players were sent to the front line. Skipper Fritz Walter was one of the few who survived. Many of his teammates, including goalscorer August Klingler, lost their lives. Walter subsequently captained the Germans to World Cup victory in 1954, under the apparently rehabilitated coach Herberger. As for the UFWC, the war finally brought international football to a standstill in November 1943. There would be no further matches until June 1945.

MATCH # 247

England 4-2 Sweden
19 November 1947

Friendly

Highbury, London

Scorers: Mortensen (3), Lawton (England),
Nordahl, Gren (pen) (Sweden)

England, Scotland, Northern Ireland, and Wales resigned from FIFA shortly before the Second World War, but all parties kissed and made up in May 1947 and a celebratory Great Britain versus the Rest of the World match was played at Hampden Park. The British side, boasting five England players, thrashed their opponents 6-1, issuing a warning to European opposition that British football was very much back in business. But UFWC champs Sweden had just gone 10 games unbeaten, scoring 51 goals along the way. That formidable goalscoring record was down to Sweden's deadly forward line of Gunnar Gren, Gunnar Nordahl, and Nils Leidholm. Both Gren and Nordahl played for the Rest of the World side at Hampden, and Nordahl scored the side's goal. So Sweden represented tough opposition for any team. Although England were hardly 'any team'. Frank Swift, George Hardwick, Wilf Mannion, and Tommy Lawton had all played for the Great Britain team, and Mannion and Lawton scored two goals each. Then there were the likes of Tom Finney, Billy Wright, and Stan Mortensen. And it was Blackpool's Mortensen who struck first at Highbury as England dominated the first half. Lawton netted a penalty, and Mortensen added a second goal to give England a 3-0 lead, but Nordahl pulled one back just before half-time to make it 3-1. Sweden rallied in the second half, and Gren scored a penalty to make the score 3-2.

Sweden pushed for an equaliser, and it seemed destined to come. Then, with just four minutes remaining, Mortensen picked up the ball on the halfway line, ran 40 yards, and drove in a magnificent goal to claim a hat-trick and a 4-2 victory. Sweden's three brilliant forwards subsequently led their country to gold at the 1948 Olympics, before signing for AC Milan and becoming known as the 'Gre-No-Li' trio. The move to Milan meant all three were forced to retire from international football due to Sweden's rule prohibiting professionals from playing for the national side. The three missed the World Cups of 1950 and 1954, but a rule rethink meant Gren and Liedholm both returned for the 1958 tournament. England temporarily lost the UFWC title to Scotland in April 1949, but regained it 12 months later. Then, for the first time ever, the UFWC holders were invited to attend the World Cup finals.

HALL OF FAME - GUNNAR NORDAHL

Centre-forward **Gunnar Nordahl** was the most prolific of Sweden and AC Milan's brilliant 'Gre-No-Li' trio. Born in 1920, Nordahl scored an amazing 44 goals in 30 games for Sweden, before his club move to Milan led to his premature international retirement. At club level he became AC Milan's all-time top scorer, netting 210 league goals in eight seasons. He was the top scorer in Serie A five times, and remains the league's all-time second highest scorer. Nordahl died in 1995.

Joe Gaetjens, US striker of 'the shot heard around the world'

MATCH # 262

England 0-1 USA
29 June 1950
World Cup finals
Estadio Independencia, Belo Horizonte, Brazil
Scorer: Gaetjens (USA)

The 1950 World Cup tournament was another organisational shambles, with withdrawals and disqualifications leaving just 13 teams playing in four uneven qualifying groups of four, four, three, and two. Germany and Japan were excluded as they were under Allied occupation, while India were refused entry as they insisted on playing barefoot. But, crucially, for the first time the UFWC holders were invited. This was UFWC champs England's first World Cup appearance, and much was expected of the so-called 'Kings of Football'. The lowly USA had lost their last seven matches and conceded 45 goals along the way. London bookies offered odds of 500-1 against a US victory. English manager Walter Winterbottom must have felt confident – he left out the great Stanley Matthews. His side still featured the likes of Alf Ramsey, Tom Finney, Wilf Mannion, and Stan Mortenson. The US side, on the other hand, contained just one professional footballer, skipper and full-back Ed McIlvenny. Goalkeeper and D-Day veteran Frank Borghi was a funeral director, centre-back Charley Colombo was a meat packer, and Haitian-born centre-forward Joe Gaetjens washed dishes in a New York restaurant. Straight from the kick-off, England, wearing unfamiliar blue shirts, peppered the US goal with shots from all distances. But the USA, organised by Scottish coach Bill Jeffrey, held firm. Then, eight minutes before half-time, US half-back Walter Bahr hit a speculative shot from almost 30 yards that English keeper Bert Williams easily had covered. Enter the dish-washing centre-forward. Joe Gaetjens dived full-length to connect with the ball and deflect it past Williams into the back of the net. England fought for an equaliser for the remaining 57 minutes, but the crowd favoured the underdogs, chanting, 'One more!' When England did break through the defence, Borghi produced heroics, including three highly un-conventional stops with his face. At the final whistle English players sunk to their knees, as jubilant spectators invaded the pitch. Goalscorer Gaetjens was carried from the stadium at shoulder height. The USA became the first side from the Ameri-cas to win the UFWC. It was the USA's greatest-ever interna-tional football result, but few Americans knew or cared. Only one US reporter saw the game – Dent McSkimming from the *St Louis Post Dispatch*. McSkimming paid for his own airfare after the paper refused to cover his expenses. 'It was like Oxford University beating the Yankees in baseball,' he wrote. Back in England, newspapers ran with black borders, with *The Daily Express* reporting that England had been 'outplayed by Ameri-can amateurs and semipros'. The US lost the UFWC title to Chile in their next game, and neither the US nor England quali-fied for the next round of the World Cup. Although the England team went on to better things, the US side was broken up and never played together again. The US players deserved more credit for their amazing victory. Goal-maker Bahr reflected, 'Nine times out of 10 they would have beaten us, but that game was our game.'

HALL OF FAME - JOE GAETJENS

United States goalscorer **Joe Gaetjens** was 26 years old when he hit 'the shot heard around the world'. Born in Haiti in 1924, Gaetjens moved to the US to study at New York's Columbia University, and worked as a restaurant dishwasher to pay his way. Renowned for his speed and style on the football pitch, he cut a distinctive figure with his socks around his ankles. Gaetjens never played for the US after 1950, but turned out for Haiti in a World Cup qualifier in 1953. He had a brief spell at Troyes in France, then returned to Haiti to open a dry cleaning business. In 1964 the apolitical Gaetjens was arrested by the Tonton Macoutes, the Haitian secret police, and was never seen again. 15 years later, the Inter-American Commission on Human Rights published a report that concluded: 'The fact that Mr Gaetjens, a football player of international standing, has not been seen since his detention in 1964 leads to the conclusion that he is dead.' Witnesses later claimed that, within days of his arrest, Gaetjens was lined up against a wall and shot.

THE UNOFFICIAL 'SOCCER' WORLD CHAMPIONS

US 'soccer' was more popular than baseball at the end of the 19th century, and the star-studded NASL briefly raised the sport's profile in the 1970s, but the beautiful game has never truly captured the hearts of American sports fans. So it should come as no surprise to learn that few US soccer fans are aware of their country's UFWC triumph. 'Hell, we Americans are barely aware of the official World Cup let alone the Unofficial Football World Championships!' said Mark Wheeler of unofficial US soccer supporters club Sam's Army. A US movie about the classic 1950 match, *Game of Their Lives* starring Patrick Stewart as reporter Dent McSkimming and Jimmy Jean-Louis as Joe Gaetjens, was released in US cinemas in 2005 to general apathy.

MATCH # 262

Chile 0-3 Brazil
20 April 1952
Pan American Championships
Estadio Nacional, Santiago, Chile
Scorers: Ademir (2), Pinga (Brazil)

Neither Brazil nor Chile won the 1950 World Cup – that honour went to Uruguay – but Brazil finished second in the tournament, and Chile came out as UFWC champions, taking the title from the USA. Brazil were UFWC virgins, having never contested the title. Both sides then went straight into the inaugural Pan American Championships, a round-robin competition involving six sides from three American continents. Hosts Chile were clear favourites, and set about their opposition in devastating style, whacking Panama 6-1 and Mexico 4-0, then seeing off Peru 3-2 and official champions Uruguay 2-0. Brazil, meanwhile, saw their reputation suffer after losing out in the World Cup. They changed their coach and training techniques, and drafted in new players to bolster their squad, but the Brazilian press and public were hardly backing their team. A stuttering start to the tournament drained confidence and hopes, but a spirited and combative win over the mighty Uruguay in the penultimate round of matches soon changed that. Suddenly, Brazil were one point behind leaders Chile going into a final decisive match between the two sides. Victory for Brazil would see them win the tournament – and the UFWC. A loss or draw would hand the glory to Chile. This time, the Brazilians did not disappoint. The match was described as a fantastic spectacle, with Brazil showing great technique and skill, and peppering the Chilean goal with shots. English referee Charles Dean had little cause to blow his whistle as the match was contested in a 'keen but fair' manner. Despite the best efforts of Chilean goalkeeper Sergio Livingstone, Brazil took a 2-0 lead into half-time courtesy of deadly Vasco da Gama forward Ademir. (Chile's star man, George 'Pancho' Robledo, was missing from their line-up, busy playing in England for Newcastle United.) The second half was all about Brazil keeping possession, but was notable for both sides making three substitutions – the Pan American Championships being one of the first competitions in the world to allow such changes. One of the Brazilian subs, Pinga of Portuguesa, popped up with a goal, and the match ended 3-0. Brazil won their first ever-international tournament in the Pan American Championships, and took the UFWC title at the first time of asking. A promising start for the international side that would go on to be one of the most successful in football history. Brazil scored 11 goals in their next three UFWC victories, but lost 1-0 to Peru in 1953.

HALL OF FAME - ADEMIR

Ademir Marques de Menezes was a quick and powerful two-footed striker, who made his name at the World Cup finals in 1950 where he won the Golden Boot by scoring nine goals. Overall, he scored 32 goals in 39 games for Brazil, including his brace in the 1952 UFWC win. Born in 1922, Ademir became known as 'Queixada', or 'Jaw', because of his prominent jawbone. At club level he played 429 times for Vasco de Gama, scoring 301 goals and winning five league championships, and also played for and won the league with Fluminese. Ademir died in 1996.

MATCH # 273

Uruguay 3-0 Peru
28 March 1953
South American Championships
National Stadium, Lima, Peru
Scorers: Peláez (2), C Romero (Uruguay)

Although Uruguay were enjoying their second reign as official world champions, having won the 1950 World Cup tournament in Brazil, the nation had never won the UFWC title. Their two UFWC attempts had resulted in defeat at the hands of Chile and Brazil. This match was part of the round robin South American Championships (known since 1975 as the Copa America), a tournament that Uruguay had previously won no less than eight times. The 1953 South American Championships was scheduled to be played in Paraguay, but the venue was changed due to concerns over the standard of that nation's stadiums. New hosts Peru went into the tournament with a Northern Irish coach. Billy Cook was a former Northern Ireland international who won the Scottish Cup with Celtic in 1931 and the FA Cup with Everton in 1933. But, after winning only one of their opening three matches, Peru dispensed with Cook's services, replacing him with Uruguayan Angel Fernández, a veteran of the 1930 World Cup-winning side. (Billy Cook went on to coach Iraq, and returned home to manage Portadown and Northern Ireland Under 23s.) Fernández's first game in charge saw controversy as 'La Blanquirroja' played out a disorderly 2-2 draw with Paraguay. The violent encounter led to Paraguay's Milner Ayala being banned from football for three years for kicking English referee Richard Maddison. The game was subsequently awarded to Peru when officials realised that Paraguay coach

Fleitas Solich had made four substitutions – one more than was allowed. Peru won their next match against Brazil 1-0 to take the UFWC title and set up an exciting finish to the South American Championships. Ironically, Angel Fernández would lead his adopted charges into battle against his home nation he served so well as a player. A win for Peru against Uruguay would give them an unassailable lead at the top of the tournament table. But the 'Charrúas' of Uruguay proved to be tough opponents. The official champions took the lead against the unofficial champs midway through the first half through Donald Peláez, a striker from Rampla Juniors. Peláez netted a second after 67 minutes, and the game was sealed four minutes later by Carlos Romero. There was another Romero on the Uruguay substitute's bench – Hosiriz 'Hos' Romero was on the books of Liverpool at the time, although he never made a first team appearance for the English club. So Uruguay were comprehensive victors, and became the undisputed football world champions as only the second team in history to simultaneously hold both the official and unofficial titles (after 1938 World Cup champs Italy won the UFWC in 1939). As for the South American Championships, this result ruined Peru's hopes, and wasn't enough for Uruguay. Both sides finished one point behind joint-leaders Brazil and Paraguay. A playoff decider saw Paraguay beat Brazil 3-2 and win the 1953 South American Championships. Uruguay would go on to hold off a challenge from England in a 2-1 friendly match victory, before losing the UFWC title to Paraguay in April 1954.

MATCH # 277

Paraguay 3-5 Argentina
2 March 1955
South American Championships
Estadio Nacional, Santiago, Chile
Scorers: Rolón, Martínez, Villalba (Paraguay),
Micheli (4), Borrello (Argentina)

The 1955 South American Championships saw all of the games played in Chile over the course of a month. Paraguay became UFWC champs in April 1954, beating Uruguay 4-1 to prevent the 1950 World Cup winners from taking the UFWC title into the 1954 World Cup finals. Neither Paraguay nor Argentina participated in those finals, so they both had plenty of time to prepare for this UFWC clash. And the resultant match was a classic. Both sides had great forward lines, so this was never going to be nil-nil. Paraguay boasted Maximo Rolón, just 5'2", but top scorer in his domestic league with Libertad three seasons running. Argentina had the brilliant Rudolfo Micheli of Independiente, one of the greatest South American goalscorers of all time. And it was Micheli who struck first – only for Rolón to grab an equaliser. Micheli then scored a penalty to give Argentina a 2-1 half-time lead. But within seconds of the start of the second half, Paraguay were also awarded a penalty. Hermes González's spot kick hit the post, but Eulogio Martínez quickly stabbed in the equaliser. (Martínez would later play for Barcelona, scoring the first ever goal in the Nou Camp stadium, and, after gaining Spanish nationality, winning eight caps for Spain.) The parity lasted less than 20 minutes. First Micheli netted a hat-trick goal, and then Boca Juniors forward Jose 'Cucumber' Borello added another to give Argentina a 4-2 lead.

(The origin of Borello's highly unusual nickname seems to have been lost to time.) Now Argentina were in control, and Micheli eventually scored his fourth – and Argentina's fifth – in the 83rd minute. Paraguay never gave up, and Salvador Villalba pulled one back with a minute left to play. But in the end Argentina, and Micheli in particular, were too strong. Argentina won 5-3 and, just as Brazil had done three years previously, they won the UFWC title at the first time of asking. Argentina successfully held onto the title throughout the remainder of the South American Championships, coming up against Chile in the final decisive match. Chile had George Robledo and his brother Ted, who had both recently returned from England to Chile with club side Colo Colo, plus Carlos Espinoza and René Meléndez, both signed to Everton. But Micheli was the man of the moment, and his single goal was enough to give Argentina the 1-0 victory that won them the 1955 South American Championships. Argentina eventually lost the UFWC title to Brazil in February 1956. The title was also won by Italy, Peru, Chile, Bolivia, and Uruguay, before West Germany took it into the 1958 World Cup finals.

HALL OF FAME – RODOLFO MICHELI

Rodolfo Micheli scored four goals to net Argentina the UFWC title in their first ever title match. Born in 1930, the right-sided Independiente forward hit eight goals in the 1955 Copa America tournament and finished as top-scorer, yet he only scored two further goals in his entire international career, including one against England in 1953.

MATCH # 328

Brazil 5-2 Sweden
29 June 1958
World Cup final
Råsunda Stadium, Solna, Sweden
Scorers: Vavá (2), Pelé (2), Zagallo (Brazil),
Liedholm, Simonsson (Sweden)

This was the first World Cup tournament to be broadcast on worldwide television, and those who tuned in were lucky enough to see a fantastic competition, notable for the birth of a classic Brazilian side, and the introduction of a genuine footballing legend. In fact, make that *two* genuine footballing legends. For alongside the great Pelé in the Brazilian ranks was the arguably greater Garrincha. Hosts and UFWC champs Sweden rebuilt their side for the tournament, following a rule change that allowed veteran pros Gunnar Gren and Nils Liedholm to return to the side after an 11-year hiatus, aged 37 and 35 respectively. Grumblings over the Scandinavian side's inclusion of professionals led to the match being billed as the Swedish mercenaries versus the Brazilian magicians. But it was a piece of Swedish magic that kicked the game into life. With just three minutes on the clock, Liedholm collected a pass from Gren and made a spectacular surge through the Brazilian rearguard. Riding challenge after challenge, Liedholm retained control and fired a wonderful shot from the edge of the area across Brazilian keeper Gilmar and into the net. The strike was later described by Pelé as the best ever scored against his side. It was the first time Brazil had been behind in the tournament, but any questions about whether they would fold or fight were swiftly answered. First Garrincha put in two low crosses and

Vavá provided two sliding finishes for a pair of remarkably similar goals. Then, in the second half, 17-year-old Pelé made his mark on the world game, taking the ball on his chest, flicking it over a defender, and volleying it home in inimitable style. Mario Zagallo scored Brazil's fourth, applying a finish to his own corner kick after the Swedes failed to clear their lines. Gren set up Agne Simonsson to pull one back with 10 minutes to play, but there was to be no way back for Sweden. In the final minute, Pelé started and finished a move that saw him head home Zagallo's looping cross. Pelé, Garrincha, and Brazil were the World Cup and UFWC champions, and indisputably the best team in the world. Brazil remained unbeaten in 11 UFWC games before Uruguay intervened in 1959. Argentina took over in 1960, but lost out to Spain in 1961. Then Spain took the title into the 1962 World Cup, where it was captured by Czechoslovakia, and then Mexico.

HALL OF FAME - GARRINCHA

Garrincha – real name **Manuel Francisco dos Santos** – was born in Pau Grande in 1933. Despite his diminutive stature – like a small wren or 'Garrincha' – and bowed left leg, he was exceptionally quick and boasted a mazy dribble. Garrincha won the World Cup twice alongside Pele in 1958 and 1962. But it was mostly downhill from there. His bowed leg weakened, and his playing career fell apart. He suffered financial problems, struggled to sustain his 13 children, killed his mother-in-law in a car accident, and sought solace from depression in drink. Garrincha fell into an alcoholic coma and died in 1983 aged 49.

MATCH # 358

Mexico 1-2 Dutch Antilles
24 March 1963
CONCACAF Cup
Estadio Flor Blanca, Santa Ana, El Salvador
Scorers: Ortíz (Mexico)
Ronald Delanoy, Jesús del Muro (o.g.) (Antilles)

So it was Mexico, one of the biggest countries in the world with a population of over 100 million, versus the Antilles, a small Dutch-claimed group of islands in the Caribbean Sea with a population of around 200,000. (The Dutch Antilles, also known as the Netherlands Antilles, previously known as the Netherlands West Indies, played as Curacao until 1948 when that island became part of the Antilles. The side's national anthem is the humbly named *Anthem Without A Title.*) Let's not underestimate the shock value of this result. FIFA rankings didn't start for another 30 years, but since they did the Antilles have never got within 100 places of Mexico. That's Mexico, established as World Cup regulars and reigning UFWC champions, versus the Antilles, who had failed to qualify for any World Cup and were UFWC virgins. This was giant killing of the very tallest order indeed. Mighty Mexico – the Tricolores – took the UFWC title during the 1962 World Cup finals from eventual finalists Czechoslovakia. The lowly Antilles, managed by Brazilian Pedro da Cunha, beat Haiti over two legs to qualify for this inaugural CONCACAF Cup tournament in El Salvador. The Confederation of North, Central American and Caribbean Association Football formed at the beginning of the year. (The CONCACAF Cup only existed in this format for five years. It has since been re-jigged and is known as the CONCACAF Gold Cup.) It was the Dutch

Antilles, or Antillas Holandesas as the Mexicans would have it, who scored first, netting through Ronald Delanoy on 12 minutes. Mexico equalised through Guillermo Ortíz 12 minutes later, and it was 1-1 at half-time. The second half was an even match-up, but there was to be an almighty sting in the tail for Mexico. With 10 minutes left to play, Mexican defender Jesús del Muro put through his own net to give the Antilles a 2-1 lead. Could the little islanders hold on? Yes they could. And the fact that Mexico gave them something of a helping hand shouldn't detract from the huge achievement of the minnows. The victorious Antilles qualified for the final round, while Mexico went out. The Antilles subsequently lost 1-0 to eventual winners Costa Rica and finished the tournament in third place. 10 years later Mexico gained some sort of revenge against the Antilles by cuffing them 8-0 in a World Cup qualifier. But giant-killers the Antilles retained their place in the record books as by far the smallest nation ever to win the UFWC. Indeed, the Antilles are the only UFWC winners with a population of under 1 million. They are also by far the lowest FIFA-ranked UFWC champs, having been ranked by FIFA as low as 188 out of 205 registered footballing nations. A true David among Goliaths. As for the UFWC, Costa Rica held the title for five matches before losing out to Colombia. Then Ecuador staged their own giant-killing act to become short-lived champions. Chile were next up, but they lost the title to the USSR who went on a 10-game unbeaten run towards the 1966 World Cup finals.

MATCH # 382

England 4-2 West Germany AET
30 July 1966
World Cup final

Wembley Stadium, England

Scorers: Hurst (3), Peters (England),

Haller, Weber (Germany)

1966 and all that was the scene of England's greatest football achievement. The USSR took the UFWC title into the 1966 World Cup tournament, but West Germany beat them 2-1 at the semi-final stage. England then saw off Portugal by the same scoreline to set up an epic encounter. For the final, 93,000 spectators crammed into Wembley Stadium, and an estimated 400 million people tuned in on TV. Then it was game on as England and West Germany contested both the World Cup and the Unofficial Football World Championships. The Germans took the lead through Helmut Haller after just 16 minutes, but England quickly struck back with a header from Geoff Hurst. Martin Peters gave England the lead in the second half, but an 89th-minute Wolfgang Weber equaliser saw the match go into extra-time. 'You've won it once, now win it again,' England manager Alf Ramsey told his side. His players didn't disappoint. Hurst's controversial crossbar/goal-line strike is still disputed to this day, but his stunning 120th-minute hat-trick goal could not be denied. England won the World Cup and, some might say more importantly, the UFWC to become the undisputed official and unofficial football world champions. TV viewers were treated to commentator Kenneth Wolstenholme's legendary proclamation, 'Some people are on the pitch. They think it's all over... It is now!' and then, as Bobby Moore lifted the Jules Rimet trophy, 'It is only 12 inches high... It is solid gold... And it undeniably means England are the champions of the world!' The victorious players were whisked off to a boozy reception at the Royal Garden Hotel in Kensington. PM Harold Wilson was in attendance wearing a World Cup tie, but the guest of honour was Pickles, the two-year-old mongrel who found the trophy under a hedge after it was stolen by mysterious thief 'The Pole'. Amid the post match celebrations, German goalscorer Haller nicked the match ball, but kindly returned it to hat-trick hero Hurst a full 30 years later – after *The Mirror* newspaper coughed up £80,000. But let it be noted that not all Germans were ungracious in defeat. The *Bild am Sontag* reported, 'England are 1966 world champions. Bravo. The players from the Motherland have done it for the first time.' Many years after the event a group of boffins at Oxford University used computers to prove that Hurst's second goal had not, in fact, crossed the line. No one in England cared one jot.

HALL OF FAME - TOFIK BAKHRAMOV

The so-called 'Russian linesman' famed for allowing Geoff Hurst's second goal and upsetting an awful lot of Germans, was actually from Azerbaijan. **Tofik Bakhramov** was a legendary football figure in his home country, and a well-respected international referee. Born in 1926, Bakhramov turned to officiating after injury ruined his playing career. He once described matches as duels, 'full of unforeseen turns and even real miracles.' In 2004 a grateful Hurst unveiled a statue of Bakhramov, who died in 1993, next to Azerbaijan's Tofik Bakhramov National Stadium.

MATCH # 383

Northern Ireland 0-2 England
22 October 1966
European Championships qualifier
Windsor Park, Belfast
Scorers: Hunt, Peters

The combined World Cup champions and Unofficial Football World Championships title-holders returned to action for the first time in this combined European Championships qualifier and British Home Championships match. It was decided that the six matches of the 1966-67 BHC and the six matches of the 1967-68 BHC involving England, Ireland, Scotland, and Wales would also serve as the 12 matches of 1968 European Championships qualifying group 8. This, of course, rendered the BHC virtually worthless, but it did mean that this match combined three competitions – the BHC, the EC, and the UFWC. Alf Ramsey, unsurprisingly, saw no need to reshuffle his side, and England lined up with the 11 players that had won the World Cup. By contrast, Northern Ireland drew many of their players from lower league sides, but the side was not without its star men – among the Irish 11 were controversial striker Doug 'Doog' Dougan, then at Leicester City, and a 20-year-old Belfast boy named George Best. Best was already a legend – six months earlier he had scored two goals in the first 10 minutes of the European Cup quarter-final match against Benfica to inspire Manchester United to a 5-1 win. But he had spent the summer recovering from a cartilage operation, and had only just got back to match fitness. Northern Ireland managed to keep the visitors at bay until the 40th minutes, when Roger Hunt scored. At half-time, injured Northern Ireland goalkeeper

Pat Jennings was substituted and replaced between the sticks by Willie McFaul. 15 minutes into the second half, McFaul was forced to pick the ball out of his net after Martin Peters scored a second goal. Willie Ferguson was sent off for Northern Ireland, but the game finished 2-0. England remained undisputed official and unofficial champions.

HALL OF FAME - GEORGE BEST

Perhaps the greatest footballer of all time, **George Best** famously never graced the World Cup finals, but he did play in a UFWC title match, albeit a defeat. Born in 1946, Best scored 9 goals in 37 games for Northern Ireland. Dubbed the 'fifth Beatle', his celebrity lifestyle led to problems with gambling, women, and alcohol. 'I spent a lot of money on booze, birds, and fast cars,' he famously remarked, 'the rest I just squandered.' Ultimately, his career and his life were cut short by alcoholism. Best died in 2005 aged just 59. 'Pelé called me the greatest footballer in the world,' he once said. 'That is the ultimate salute to my life.'

HALL OF FAME - BOBBY MOORE

Robert Frederick Chelsea Moore OBE was born in 1941, and made his name as a cultured defender at West Ham United. His crowning moment came in 1966 when he skippered his country to World Cup and UFWC glory. Renowned as a gentleman and fair player, Moore nevertheless experienced problems off the field. Framed for stealing a bracelet in Bogota in 1970, Moore was later accused of raiding his teammates' lockers during a 1974 charity match in Dusseldorf. Despite his World Cup win, Moore died in 1993 having never received a knighthood.

'Slim Jim' Baxter, the architect of a famous Scottish victory

MATCH #386

England 2-3 Scotland
15 April 1967
European Championships qualifier
Wembley Stadium, London
Scorers: J Charlton, Hurst (England)
Law, Lennox, McCalliog (Scotland)

This was the match that cemented the idea of an unofficial championship in the minds of many Scottish football fans. 30,000 members of the Tartan Army travelled to Wembley to see their side take on World Cup Champions and UFWC holders England. To say that England were clear favourites would be an understatement. The Auld Enemy had not lost a match since 1965, and were being referred to as 'The Invincibles'. Scotland had failed to even qualify for the 1966 tournament that England won so memorably. 'On the surface at least, we had no reason to feel confident,' said Scottish captain John Greig, 'but we had considered ourselves unfortunate not to qualify for the 1966 finals and we were desperate to make a point.' New Scottish manager Bobby Brown could not have chosen a more daunting match for first game in charge. As he delivered his pre-match team-talk, Brown was surprised to see cheeky midfielder Jim Baxter engrossed in the *Daily Telegraph*. Nonplussed, Brown asked, 'Anything to add, Jim?' 'Aye,' replied Baxter. 'See this English lot, they can play nane.' Baxter's words summed up his side's confident team spirit. Indeed, Scotland outplayed England by a greater margin than the score might suggest. Denis Law scored Scotland's first goal within half an hour, but it was Baxter who was running the game. 'Slim Jim' at one point played 'keepy-uppy' near the corner flag, such was the Scottish dominance. On 78 minutes, Bobby Lennox added a second goal. But perhaps the Scots were overplaying. Jack Charlton pulled one back for the English with six minutes left to play. Then, with three minutes left, James McCalliog scored a third for Scotland. England went straight back up the field for Geoff Hurst to score, but Scotland held on to win 3-2. The Tartan Army invaded the Wembley pitch and scooped up handfuls of turf to take home as souvenirs. 'The English players were far too cocky!' explained John Greig. Crucially, in claiming at the time to be unofficial champions on account of beating the World Cup winners, Scottish football fans sowed the statistical seed that grew to become what is now the UFWC. Scotland *were* now the Unofficial Football World Champions. This had been another combined EC qualifier and BHC match. Scotland won the 1966-67 BHC, but finished second in the 1967-68 BHC, ultimately missing out on European Championships qualification by a single point to England.

HALL OF FAME - JIM BAXTER

James Curran Baxter was a drunk, a womaniser, a gambler, and a footballing genius. Blessed with great skill and no little confidence, he could do pretty much anything with his brilliant left foot. His teammates, he reckoned 'weren't fit to lick me boots'. He made 34 appearances for Scotland, and played at club level for Raith Rovers, Rangers, Sunderland, and Nottingham Forest. Born in 1939, 'Slim Jim' died of cancer in 2001, after which Scottish fans launched a cheeky attempt to get England's new Wembley Stadium footbridge named in his honour.

SCOTLAND - UNOFFICIALLY THE BEST

Few sets of fans have had as much cause to celebrate the Unofficial Football World Championships as Scotland's Tartan Army. Not only did their side's 1967 victory over arch rivals and official world champions England do much to inspire the unofficial competition, but, according to the UFWC rankings table, Scotland are unofficially the best team in the world. Scotland top the rankings table, a full 11 points ahead of second-placed England. It's clear that both nations are so highly ranked because of their dominance of international football in the years that preceded the first World Cup. (Indeed, Scotland have not actually held the title since 1967.) Detractors say this isn't fair, as other nations weren't around to challenge for the title in football's formative years. But a key attribute of the UFWC is that its lineage goes right back to the very beginning of international football. Other nations came late to the table, after Scotland and England had already gouged themselves on the beautiful game. So Scotland top the rankings on merit, despite the protestations of rival fans. 'What a piss-take!' complained Englishman D Plant to the UFWC website. 'It's obvious that the UFWC came about thanks to a disgruntled Scot clinging to a set of statistics and an anorak!' (In fact, none of the UFWC originators are Scottish.) In the absence of anything official to celebrate, the Tartan Army responded to news of Scotland's unofficial title in typically good humoured and self-deprecating fashion. 'I'm all for anything that makes us look better than we are!' said Tam Ferry of the Association of Tartan Army Clubs. The Scottish FA seemed slightly less enthusiastic. 'It is certainly a good bit of fun,' commented SFA head of communication Andy Mitchell. 'But really, we are more concerned about the team of today and getting to major championships.' Good luck with that, but for now Scotland can enjoy their UFWC success.

MATCH #397

Austria 1-1 Greece
(match abandoned but score stands)
5 November 1967
European Championships qualifier

Vienna

Scorers: Siber (Austria)

Sideris (Greece)

On paper this match should not have offered much to get excited about. The last Group 3 qualifying match for the 1968
European Championships was effectively meaningless, as the
USSR had already secured the only qualifying spot at the top of
the table. To the uninformed observer, Austria and Greece were
playing for nothing but pride, and certainly the match was very
ordinary for the first 84 minutes. But, unbeknown to those
involved, there was something important at stake – the not-
inconsequential matter of the UFWC title. And, in the 85th
minute on the 5th of November, fireworks duly erupted, ensur-
ing the match would go down in history as one of the strangest
ever played. Helmut Siber of German club Kickers Offenbach
struck after 32 minutes to give title-holders Austria a first half
lead. Free-scoring Olympiakos striker Giorgios Sideris pulled
Greece level in the 73rd minute, but the match only really
came to life amid late controversy. With just five minutes left to
play, referee Mr Gere of Hungary saw fit to send off Greece's
star player, Takis Loukanidis. For the record, Panathinaikos's
footballing all-rounder Loukandis is now considered one of
Greece's best ever players and was regarded at the time as
something approaching a living Greek God. Inevitably, the
Greek contingent in the crowd was enraged, and mindless

mayhem immediately erupted. Scores of spectators, apparently of both Greek and Austrian persuasion, charged onto the pitch and began to engage in a mass brawl. Players from both sides were caught up and became involved in furious fistfights, while ref Gere was unceremoniously bashed over the head with a bottle. A full-scale riot was underway, and 200 Austrian policemen, with horses, dogs, and big sticks, were sent onto the pitch to put an end to it. Order was eventually restored but there was no sensible way that play could continue, so the match was abandoned. In the aftermath of the riot the Austrian authorities were severely reprimanded, and UEFA threatened to make Austria play all fixtures away from home if such an incident ever happened again. But what made the case particularly unusual was UEFA's decision not to order a replay. UEFA declared that the 1-1 score should stand, even though the match had not been completed. The fact that the result had no effect on European Championships qualification probably had some bearing on the decision. As, no doubt, did the possibility of another riot. This was only the second UFWC title match in history to be abandoned (the other being the Ibrox disaster of 1902), but the score nevertheless stands for UFWC purposes, as it does for official FIFA records. Not that the 1-1 draw changed the titleholders or ranking points, with Austria retaining the title for another seven months before losing 3-1 to the USSR. Sweden, France, and Switzerland were subsequent winners, with Switzerland failing to qualify for the 1970 World Cup finals. But the UFWC title would be contested at the official tournament in 1974.

MATCH # 444

Netherlands 2-0 Brazil
3 July 1974
World Cup finals
Westfalenstadion, Dortmund, West Germany
Scorers: Neeskens, Cruyff (Netherlands)

Unofficial champs the Netherlands went into this World Cup tournament game unbeaten in 14 UFWC matches. Brazil were official champions and pretty much dominated the world game since the 50s. But more than a match between unofficial and official champions, this was a clash between two of the most skilful and entertaining sides football had ever produced. The Dutch were all about total football – pioneered by coach Rinus Michels, and personified by captain Johan Cruyff. Their tasty side also contained the likes of Johan Neeskens, Johnny Rep, and Ruud Krol. The Brazilians played Samba Soccer – showing legendary beach-honed skill and technique. Although Pelé and Carlos Alberto had left the scene, the likes of Jairzinho and Rivelino were very much still around. This was the final second round group match, and essentially a World Cup semi-final. The Netherlands needed a draw to top their group and proceed to the final. But a win for Brazil would see them leapfrog the Dutch and go through. Regrettably, the Netherlands's brilliant orange and Brazil's golden yellow first choice shirts were deemed to clash, so the sides lined up in unfamiliar white and blue respectively. Lacking their most illustrious stars *and* their famous yellow kit, Brazil didn't quite look like the team adored by football fans around the world. Neither did they play like them. Despite the promise of skill and technique, the first half was a tale of missed opportunities and bad tackles – mostly from the surprisingly brutal Brazilians. But Brazil's attempts at kicking, tripping, and stamping on the Dutch were to no avail. Five minutes after the restart Neeskens met a Cruyff cross at the near post and poked it expertly over Brazilian keeper Emerson Leao. The confident Dutch retained possession of the ball, and struck again after 65 minutes. Krol's cross from the left was met with a flying volley from the onrushing Cruyff, who deflected the ball into the net with an outstretched right boot. The frustrated Brazilians had no way back, and the game was effectively over when Luis Pereira was sent off for kicking away Neeskens's legs. The Netherlands went to meet West Germany in the World Cup final, and Brazil went home. The Brazilians would in later years reclaim the UFWC and the World Cup, but for now their dominance of world football was over.

HALL OF FAME - JOHAN CRUYFF

Hendrik Johannes Cruijff, or Cruyff, was named European Footballer of the Year three times, but the UFWC was the only international title he won in his 48 games for his country. A difficult genius, Cruyff ruined the Dutch squad's unique alphabetic numbering system for the 1974 World Cup by demanding to wear his trademark number 14 shirt. The Puma-sponsored star also refused to wear Adidas's trademark three stripes on his shirtsleeves, playing in a specially altered two-stripe strip. He didn't turn up at all for the World Cup in 1978, in protest against the Argentinean Junta. Born in 1947, at club level Cruyff played for and managed Ajax and Barcelona. A former 20-a-day smoker, he swapped cigarettes for lollipops in 1991 after undergoing a double heart bypass.

MATCH # 445

West Germany 2-1 Netherlands
7 July 1974
World Cup final
Olympiastadion, Munich
Scorers: Breitner (pen), Muller (West Germany)
Neeskens (pen) (Netherlands)

Euro champions West Germany took on UFWC champions the Netherlands in a World Cup final. While the brilliant Dutch practised free-flowing total football, the formidable Germans favoured a more guarded mobile sweeper system. Hosts West Germany also had the crowd on their side, not to mention the likes of Franz Beckenbauer, Sepp Maier, Paul Breitner, and the free-scoring Gerd Muller. Kick-off in soccer's showpiece final was delayed for several minutes as groundstaff in the Olympiastadion had neglected to set up corner flags. But when play finally got underway, West Germany didn't seem ready. Indeed, the Netherlands took the lead before a German player touched the ball. Johan Cruyff strolled from his own half through the German defence and into the penalty area, only to be scythed down by Uli Hoeness. Ref Jack Taylor awarded a penalty, causing German libero Beckenbauer to point out, quite accurately, 'You're an Englishman!' The Dutch penalty-taker was the deadly Johan Neeskens, who dispatched the ball into the centre of the goal with minimum fuss. It was a very early kick in the teeth for the Germans, but they stuck to their patient gameplan – and it paid off 25 minutes later. Bernd Holzenbein squeezed into the Dutch penalty area and was challenged rather innocuously by Wim Jansen. Holzenbein went down like a sniper had taken him out. Jack Taylor again pointed to the spot. Had Beckenbauer's earlier comment persuaded Taylor to 'even the score'? Regardless, Paul Breitner buried the penalty – after Cruyff instructed keeper Jan Jongbloed to dive in the wrong direction. West Germany had the initiative, and just before half-time they had the lead. Muller turned in the box, and knocked the ball past the static Jongbloed. It was Muller's 14th World Cup goal, making him the tournament's all-time top goalscorer. The Dutch were rattled – as the half-time whistle blew Cruyff took his turn at berating ref Taylor, and was booked for his indiscretion. The Netherlands regrouped after the break and piled pressure on the German goal, but to no avail. The final whistle was greeted with delirium from the home fans. West Germany reclaimed the UFWC and, for the second time, won the World Cup. They were presented with the brand new FIFA World Cup trophy, the earlier Jules Rimet trophy having been handed permanently to three-time winners Argentina. The Germans held off UFWC challengers Switzerland, Greece, and Malta in subsequent months, then, in March 1975, played out a UFWC rematch with England – and lost 2-0.

HALL OF FAME - PAUL BREITNER

Paul Breitner scored in two World Cup finals, despite playing as a defensive midfielder. Known as 'Der Afro' for his big curly hair, he was infamous for the straight-talking attitude that saw him dropped from the 1978 World Cup squad. After his retirement, Breitner took up acting, starring in such apparently forgotten celluloid gems as *Potato Fritz* and *Kuyonga – Murder in Africa*. He has been named among the 11 ugliest World Cup footballers by the website uglyfootballers.com.

MATCH # 464

Czechoslovakia 2-2 West Germany AET
(Czechoslovakia win 5-3 on penalties)
20 June 1976
European Championships final
Crvena Zvezda Stadium, Belgrade, Yugoslavia
Scorers: Svehlik, Dobias (Czechoslovakia)
D Muller, Halzenbein (West Germany)

This epic UFWC title match and European Championships final was ultimately decided by one of the most famous penalty kicks of all time. Czechoslovakia had held the unofficial title since taking it from England in a Euro qualifier in October 1975. Qualifying whittled 32 teams down to just four, and the final tournament began at the semi-final stage. First the Czechs beat Johan Cruyff's Netherlands 3-1, and then West Germany beat host Yugoslavia 4-2. Both semis went to extra-time. The final would go even further. West Germany lined up with the formidable Franz Beckenbauer at the heart of their side, but Czechoslovakia had a midfield legend of their own in Antonin Panenka. Indeed, the impressive Czechs took an early advantage, and led 2-1 at half-time. But the Germans – the reigning World and European champions – fought back strongly and grabbed a last-gasp equaliser through Bernd Holzenbein. The match went to extra-time, and then to penalties. Masny, Bonhof, Nehoda, Flohe, Ondrus, and Bongarts all scored their kicks. Then Juremik scored to make it 4-3 to the Czechs. Uli Hoeness needed to score to restore parity. Unfortunately, he blazed his spot kick over the crossbar. Then up stepped Panenka. If the moustachioed Bohemians Prague midfielder scored, his country would win. But in front of him was the great Josef 'Sepp' Maier. The eccentric West German keeper, with baggy shorts and over-sized gloves, had already won the 1972 European Championships and the 1974 World Cup with his country. But if Panenka was at all intimidated, he didn't show it. Panenka stepped to the ball, feigned to send Maier into a full-length dive, then coolly chipped the ball into the centre of the net. It was an extraordinary penalty kick, often imitated since, but rarely bettered. Czechoslovakia won the shoot-out 5-3, and took the UFWC title and the Euro Championships trophy. This was the first of 12 UFWC title matches to be decided by a penalty shoot-out. The Czechs held on to the title for just five months – then it was wrenched back by none other than West Germany. France, the Republic of Ireland, and Bulgaria were subsequent winners, with France taking the title into the 1978 World Cup finals in Argentina.

HALL OF FAME - ANTONIN PANENKA

Famous for his deadly free kicks and a trademark Emiliano Zapata-style moustache, **Antonin Panenka** was hailed as the 'Poet of Football' after his amazing penalty kick against West Germany. 'It wasn't something I planned,' the Czech national hero explained. 'At that moment, it just seemed the right thing to do.' A strapping attacking midfielder who played the game with a cheeky smile on his face, Panenka helped Czechoslovakia finish third in the 1980 Euro championships, and qualify for the 1982 World Cup finals. Born in Prague in 1948, Panenka retired from playing in 1987, and went on to coach Bohemians Prague.

MATCH # 488

Argentina 3-1 Netherlands AET
25 June 1978
World Cup final
River Plate Stadium, Buenos Aires, Argentina
Scorers: Kempes (2), Bertoni (Argentina)
Nanninga (Netherlands)

The Netherlands reached their second consecutive World Cup final, despite the fact that Johan Cruyff stayed at home. The hugely experienced Dutch team still featured the likes of Jonny Rep, Johan Neeskens, big keeper Jan Jongbloed, and troublesome twins Willy and Rene Van der Kerkhof. Interestingly, while the Dutch abandoned their alphabetical shirt numbering system from the 1974 tournament, the Argentineans took the idea and ran with it. So Norberto Alonso had shirt number 1, and goalkeeper Ubaldo Fillol wore shirt number 6. Shirts 2 and 10, meanwhile, belonged respectively to the great pair Ossie Ardiles and Mario Kempes. Argentina grew in strength and confidence as the tournament progressed, beating Peru 6-0 in their final second round match. The Netherlands had beaten Italy 2-1 to win a place in the final, and to deprive the Italians of the UFWC title. The final match was by no means a classic, but it was a hard fought contest illuminated by flashes of brilliance. The Dutch began brightly, but it was Argentina who took the lead, with the long-haired Kempes nipping in to slide the ball past Jongbloed on 37 minutes. The second half was a midfield battle, short of excitement until the 82nd minute. Dutch coach Ernst Happel gambled on introducing substitute Dick Nanninga, and the gamble paid off as Nanninga rose highest to head home a right wing cross. The Dutch were level, and the vast majority of the 71,483 spectators were silenced. As the final whistle approached, the ball fell at the feet of Rob Resenbrink, but the Dutch striker saw his shot come back off Fillol's post. The Argentineans greeted the end of the 90 minutes with relief, and gathered around coach Cesar Luis Menotti for a rallying call ahead of extra-time. Whatever Menotti said, it seemed to do the trick. Argentina were a better team in extra-time, while the Dutch seemed edgy and nervous, perhaps fearing that a second consecutive World Cup final defeat would be too much to bear. Argentina took the initiative, and got their reward midway through the extra period, with Kempes stumbling into the area, poking the ball against Jongbloed, and tapping in the rebound. Four minutes from time, Daniel Bertoni swept home Argentina's third to seal the World Cup and UFWC victory. As skipper Daniel Passarella held aloft the World Cup trophy, two words on the stadium scoreboard confirmed that a nation's dream had come true: 'Argentina Campeon!'

HALL OF FAME - MARIO KEMPES

Mario Alberto Kempes finished the 1978 World Cup finals tournament with a winners' medal and the golden boot, ending up with six goals despite failing to score at all in the first round. Born in Cordoba in 1954, Kempes spent part of his club career in Spain with Valencia, where he was nicknamed El Matador. He played in three World Cups, and scored 20 goals in 43 appearances for Argentina. He remains a living legend in his home country, and now works as an ESPN television pundit.

MATCH # 532

Italy 3-1 West Germany
11 July 1982
World Cup final
Santiago Bernabeu Stadium, Madrid, Spain
Scorers: Rossi, Tardelli, Altobelli (Italy),
Breitner (West Germany)

Spain 82 saw another UFWC / World Cup final double-header. Bolivia, Paraguay, Chile, Brazil, and Uruguay had all been UFWC champs since 1978. The title was taken into the 1982 tournament by Peru, then snatched by Poland, and then won by Italy at the semi-final stage. West Germany saw off France on penalties in their semi – an epic match overshadowed by a brutal foul by German keeper Harald Schumacher on French defender Patrick Battison. That controversy, coupled with grumbles over an alleged fixed first round match between West Germany and Austria that saw both sides cruise through to the next round, meant that few neutrals were cheering on the Germans. Italy had beaten Brazil and Argentina in the second round, and boasted the likes of Dino Zoff, Guiseppe Bergomi, Marco Tardelli, and Paolo Rossi in their side. But the Germans had held England to a draw and beaten Spain in their second round games, and also had an impressive line-up including Schumacher, Paul Breitner, Pierre Littbarski, and Karl-Heinz Rummenigge. Few would have argued against the fact that Italy and West Germany were the best teams in the tournament. But which would come out on top in front of 90,000 spectators and millions of TV viewers? West Germany enjoyed the best of the opening exchanges, but an Italian defence marshalled by Zoff and Bergomi held firm. And, after successfully soaking up the German pressure, Italy broke upfield and won a penalty. Antonio Cabrini stepped up to take the kick – but blasted the ball wide of Schumacher's right-hand post. In the second half, Italy began to show their superior technical ability and, in the 57th minute, Claudio Gentile's curling cross eluded everyone but Rossi, whose stopping header shot past Schumacher to make the score 1-0. With the Germans now forced to push forward in search of an equaliser, Italy exploited gaps at the back. First Rossi and Gaetano Scirea combined brilliantly to set up Tardelli, who scored with a low drive. Then a surging run from Conti set up Alessandro Altobelli, who side-stepped Schumacher and scored a third. Breitner pulled one back for West Germany with a drive from the edge of the area with seven minutes left to play, but his muted celebration suggested that the Germans knew it was nothing more than a consolation. Italy were champions, officially, unofficially, and indisputably.

HALL OF FAME - PAOLO ROSSI

The 1982 World Cup finals belonged to **Paolo Rossi**, who took home a winners' medal, the Golden Boot, and the Golden Ball. He also shot his side to the unofficial title, although there was no UFWC trophy to further burden his suitcase. Rossi was subsequently named European Football of the Year. Yet Italian coach Enzo Bearzot's decision to include him in the squad was highly controversial – Rossi had only just returned to football two months previously following a two-year match-fixing ban. He has always protested his innocence. Born in 1956, Rossi played 48 times for Italy, scoring 20 goals.

MATCH # 552

France 2-0 Spain
27 June 1984
European Championships final
Parc des Princes, Paris, France
Scorers: Platini, Bellone (France)

Free-scoring France took the UFWC title from Belgium in the first round of the 1984 European Championships with a 5-0 win. The tournament hosts then saw off Yugoslavia and Portugal, both defeated 3-2, to reach the final. Spain qualified for the tournament courtesy of one of the most ludicrous results ever recorded. Needing to beat Malta by a full 11 goals in their final qualifying match, Spain proceeded to miss a penalty, concede a goal, and still win 12-1. It was very difficult to imagine that the handing over of brown envelopes had not occurred, although UEFA and FIFA accepted the result. For the final, France fielded what is perhaps their classic side, featuring the peerless midfield quartet of Michel Platini, Jean Tigana, Alain Giresse, and Luis Fernandez. If they had a weakness, it was that they did not have a prolific goalscorer up front. On paper, Spain had an inferior side, with future coach Jose Antonio Camacho one of the few notable names. They scraped through to the final, winning only one first round match, and beating Denmark on penalties in the semi-final. Crucially, however, they proved difficult to beat. Approaching the final in a similarly obstinate style, the Spaniards were able to frustrate the French, and the vast majority of the 47,000 crowd, in a goalless first half. But, on 57 minutes, France won a free-kick on the edge of Spain's D. Up stepped set piece maestro Platini. But he did not produce his vintage. His free kick was lobbed weakly straight at Spanish keeper Luis Arconada. But, inexplicably, Arconada fumbled the ball and allowed it to slip over the line. Platini had broken the deadlock, with something of an assist from the goalie. Spain began probing forward in search of an equaliser, and France were reduced to 10 men after defender Yvon Le Roux was sent off, but the French midfield retained control of the game. In the final minute Bruno Bellone raced clear of the Spanish defence and chipped the ball over Arconada to seal the victory. It was France's twelfth UFWC win, but the first time the nation had ever won an official competition.

HALL OF FAME - MICHEL PLATINI

Elegant midfielder **Michel Platini** was perhaps the best passer of the ball the beautiful game has ever seen. He was also a deadly free-kick specialist, and an incredibly prolific goalscorer. 'He could thread the ball through the eye of a needle, as well as finish,' remarked Bobby Charlton. Born in 1955, Platini scored a remarkable 41 goals in 72 games from midfield for France. After skippering his country to European Championships and UFWC glory in 1984 he was appointed a Knight of the Legion of Honour. He was voted European Footballer of the Year three times in a row in 1983, 1984, and 1985, and World Player of the Year in 1984 and 1985. He later managed France, but failed to match his successes as a player. Like many of football's greatest players, Platini never won the World Cup but he can at least add the UFWC title to his impressive list of honours.

MATCH # 572

West Germany 2-3 Argentina
29 June 1986
World Cup final
Aztec Stadium, Mexico City, Mexico
Scorers: Rummenigge, Voller (West Germany),
Brown, Valdano, Burruchaga (Argentina)

Tumultuous earthquakes killed 20,000 people in Mexico in the run-up to the 1986 World Cup tournament, but the magnificent Aztec Stadium remained standing, and the football went ahead. West Germany took the UFWC title into the tournament, but lost it to Denmark in the opening round. The title was then passed to Spain, then Belgium, and then Argentina over the course of a week. Argentina reached the final largely courtesy of Diego Maradona's brilliance and cheek, famously seeing off England in the quarter-finals with an assist from the 'Hand of God', and then beating Belgium in the semis. West Germany got a chance to regain the World Cup and the UFWC after beating hosts Mexico on penalties, and then knocking out an excellent French team with a 2-0 win. The Germans had strengthened their side since losing out in the 1982 final. Alongside Harald Schumacher and Karl-Heinz Rummenigge were Lothar Mathaus, Andy Brehme, and Rudi Voller. Their coach was a man who knew all about winning the World Cup and the UFWC title – Franz 'Der Kaiser' Beckenbauer. The Germans were favourites, but the Argentineans were sure to give them a game. Although Maradona was certainly the star of the show, Argentina were anything but a one-man team. They had top goalkeeper Neri Pumpido, plus the likes of Oscar Ruggeri, Jorge Valdano, and Jorge Burruchaga. Burruchaga, or 'El Burro', was a particularly gifted attacking midfielder who surely would have been more highly regarded had he not been somewhat over-shadowed by the great Maradona. And while Maradona was instrumental in the match, Argentina delivered a true team performance. The Germans gave the job of marking Maradona to Matthaus. But Matthaus's foul on Maradona midway through the first half led to the first goal, when Burruchaga's free kick was misjudged by Schumacher, and Argentinean defender Jose Luis Brown headed home. 10 minutes after the interval Argentina doubled their lead, after Maradona and Enrique set up Valdano to score. But the Germans were never going to give up without a fight, and they struck back from two Brehme corner kicks. First Voller flicked on for Rummenigge to score, then Voller himself headed in an equaliser. With just five minutes remaining, the match was heading for extra-time. Then Maradona poked a great ball through to Burruchaga. El Burru raced clear of the German defence and slipped the ball under Schumacher to score the winner. The underdogs had pulled off a famous and deserved victory.

HALL OF FAME – JORGE BURRUCHAGA

Jorge Luis Burruchaga played 59 times for Argentina, scoring 13 goals, mostly from midfield. Born in 1962, 'El Burru' scored his country's winning goal in the 1986 World Cup final / UFWC title match, and also played at the 1990 World Cup finals. He played most of his club football for Independiente in Argentina and FC Nantes in France. He is now the coach of Estudiantes de la Plata in his home country.

MATCH # 581

Italy 0-1 Wales
4 June 1988
Friendly

Mario Rigamenti Stadium, Brescia, Italy

Scorer: Rush (Wales)

UFWC champs Italy played this warm-up friendly just six days before their opening match in the 1988 European Champion-ships. The Italians had taken the unofficial title from official world champions Argentina 12 months previously. They then went on an eight-game unbeaten run, defeating Yugoslavia, Sweden, Portugal, and the USSR along the way. Skipper Guiseppe Bergomi was a veteran of the 1982 World Cup win-ning side, and he was surrounded by a new generation of stars including Paolo Maldini, Franco Baresi, Roberto Mancini, and Gianluca Vialli. Wales had fewer star names, with Second Divi-sion Hull City's Tony Norman deputising for keeper Neville Southall, and midfielder Kevin Davies drafted in from Fourth Division Swansea City. But up front Wales had true interna-tional class in Mark Hughes and Ian Rush. Hughes was plying his trade in Germany with Bayern Munich, while skipper Rush was having a less happy time in Italy with Juventus. Rush failed to settle in Italy, and was considered to be something of a flop. But on this night Italy would see the real Ian Rush. Wales, playing in yellow, were scarcely in the game for the first 37 minutes, with Italy looking superior in every department. Then the Welsh won a throw-in near to Italy's right-hand corner flag. Everton's Pat Van den Hauwe launched a long throw into the box, Hughes peeled away to draw out the defence, and Rush received the ball at the near post, spun around, and rifled it into the far corner. The 30,000-strong crowd was stunned into silence. Italy attempted to bounce back, with Vialli, Mancini, and Altobelli all going close. But, with the indignant whistling of their supporters ringing in their ears, they could not find an equaliser. Despite having proved his worth to the Italians in dramatic style, Rush re-joined Liverpool later in the summer. Italy went to the Euro Championships in West Germany and reached the semi-finals. Wales, meanwhile, lost the UFWC title to the Netherlands courtesy of a 1-0 defeat in their very next match. Italy recaptured the title, before Romania, Poland, Sweden, Denmark, Belgium, Greece, and Portugal all enjoyed spells as unofficial champions.

HALL OF FAME - IAN RUSH

It is often said that **Ian James Rush** never got the chance to represent his country at a major international tournament, but he did skipper his side to UFWC glory, scoring the goal that secured the title in 1988. Born in 1961, Rush scored 28 goals in 73 games for Wales, and at club level scored 346 goals in 658 games for Liverpool. During his largely unsuccessful year at Juventus, a homesick Rush described Italy as being 'just like a foreign country' and had parcels of baked beans shipped over to remind him of England. He was famously name-checked in a legendary Milk Marketing Board TV commercial in which two young Scousers debate the merits of the white stuff: 'It's what Ian Rush drinks.' 'Ian Rush?' 'Yeah, and he says if I don't drink lots of milk, when I grow up I'm only gonna be good enough to play for Accrington Stanley!' 'Accrington Stanley? Who are they?' *'Exactly!'*

MATCH # 617

USA 0-1 Australia
13 June 1992
Friendly

Citrus Bowl, Orlando, USA

Scorer: Spink (Australia)

Despite traditionally preferring their footballs to be egg-shaped, the Americans were enjoying their second stint as UFWC champions, having taken the title from Portugal and held off Italy in friendly matches in Chicago earlier in the month. Australia, another country that preferred its football to be played by alternative rules – and was yet to fully embrace the beautiful game despite having been on the international stage since 1922, had never played in a UFWC title match. The match was the first of a 'goodwill series' across the Americas designed to give Australia's Socceroos match practice ahead of World Cup qualifiers. Among the US players were keeper Tony Meola, defender Marcelo Balboa, and Dutch-born striker Earnie Stewart, all of whom would play for their country in World Cup finals. The US were coached by Yugoslav Velibor 'Bora' Milutinovic. Australia's coach, Eddie Thomson, was a Scot. The Aussie line-up included controversial midfielder Ned Zelic, and defender Tony Vidmar, who would both later have relatively unsuccessful stints in England, with QPR and Middlesbrough respectively. Vidmar, Australia's most-capped player, also played for Rangers and Cardiff City. In a muggy and humid Orlando, 17,500 fans braved a huge thunderstorm to get to the game, but the kick-off was delayed for fear that the players would be struck by lightning. Indeed the match was on the verge of being abandoned, when the storm finally passed, and the go-ahead was given. In slippery conditions, neither side served up much to convince those gathered there that the game had been worth braving the weather. It was a full 85 minutes before the deadlock was broken, with Warren Spink netting the only goal of the game for the Socceroos. Australia took the UFWC title, but lost it in their next 'goodwill' match to Argentina.

HALL OF FAME - NED ZELIC

Trouble-making UFWC-winning Aussie midfielder **Ned Zelic**'s international career was short-lived after an ill-advised 'blue' with coach Frank Farina precipitated his international retirement. Enigmatic and unpredictable, Zelic, of Croatian origin, was signed for £1.3 million by Queens Park Rangers manager Ray Wilkins, who described him as 'as versatile as an egg'. But the signing was a rotten one – Zelic played only three times for the relegation bound club, suffering persistent knee injuries and eventually deciding that London wasn't for him. In 1999, after scoring a long-range goal for the Socceroos against a FIFA 'World Star' XI, he patted beaten keeper Jorge Campos on the head and called him 'short stuff'. Born in 1971, Zelic now plays for Newcastle United Jets.

UNOFFICIAL SOCCEROO WORLD CHAMPIONS

Sports-mad Australia has only recently fell in love with soccer, having traditionally played football under 'Aussie rules'. The Australians have played three UFWC title matches, but won only one. 'That's one more than Norway or Turkey or Croatia,' pointed out Socceroo fan Wayne Coupland. 'Oz will dominate football sooner or later. Watch out UFWC.'

MATCH # 630

Argentina 2-1 Mexico
4 July 1993
Copa America final
Monumental, Guayaquil, Ecuador
Scorers: Batistuta (2) (Argentina),
Galindo (pen) (Mexico)

UFWC champs Argentina played out the 1993 Copa America tournament without one Diego Armando Maradona, who had recently controversially walked out on his club side Sevilla after a disappointing season. Maradona had been dropped from the national side after being handed a 15-month ban for failing a drugs test in 1991. He would return to fail another drugs test at the 1994 World Cup, but in the meantime Argentina could rely upon other star names. Sergio Goycochea was a formidable goalkeeper, Oscar Ruggeri kept things together at the back, Fernando Redondo and Diego Simone ran the midfield, and Gabriel Batistuta was a bona fide goal machine. Mexico also had a celebrated goalkeeper in flamboyant free kick expert Jorge Campos. A fan of gaudy luminous kits, Campos managed to score more than 30 goals during his career as a netminder. Ramon Ramirez was Mexico's key defender, and Alberto Garcia Aspe ran the midfield. Up front was a man widely regarded as the best Mexican footballer of all time, the great Hugo Sanchez, famous almost as much for his back-flipping celebrations as for his many goals. Argentina had held the UFWC title for 12 straight games, having taken it from Australia. Mexico, with a poor UFWC record for such a famous footballing nation, had held the title only once, in 1962 – and then lost it to the Dutch Antilles. Argentina reached the Copa America final by beating

Brazil and Colombia in penalty shoot-outs in the quarter and semi-finals. Mexico, playing their first Copa America tournament, saw off Peru and hosts Ecuador. The game was a tight one, and it only really came to life midway through the second half. Fiorentina striker Batistuta gave Argentina the lead in the 63rd minute. 'Batigol' finished the previous Copa America as top scorer, but this was only his second strike of this tournament. Four minutes later Mexico were level, with Benjamin Galindo slotting a penalty past renowned spot kick-stopper Goycochea. But Batistuta restored Argentina's advantage in the 74th minute, and his goal proved to be decisive. Argentina won the Copa America and retained the UFWC title. They would lose the latter in the following month courtesy of a World Cup qualifier defeat to Colombia.

HALL OF FAME - GABRIEL BATISTUTA

Gabriel Omar Batistuta is Argentina's greatest ever goalscorer, netting 56 times in 78 international games. 'Batigol' was born in 1969 as the son of a slaughterhouse worker. A promising basketball player, Batistuta turned his talents to football after being inspired by the 1978 Argentinean World Cup-winning team. He scored 10 goals at three World Cup tournaments, but won only the 1993 Copa America with his country. At club level he scored 168 goals for Serie A side Fiorentina, and the city of Florence erected a bronze statue in his honour. He later won Serie A with Roma. Batigol retired from football in 2005 aged 36. Something of a sex symbol, and once described by The Observer as a 'straightforward lust-monkey', Batistuta won female hearts as an apparent footballing rarity – a family man dutifully faithful to his wife Irena.

MATCH # 651

Colombia 2-0 Switzerland
26 June 1994
World Cup finals
Stanford Stadium, Palo Alto, USA
Scorers: Gaviria, Lozano (Colombia)

The 1994 World Cup finals tournament was a miserable one for Colombia, although their on-field failings would be hugely over-shadowed by a shocking off-field tragedy. Much was expected of a Colombian team including Afro-wearing midfield maestro Carlos Valderrama, goalscoring playmaker Fredy Rincon, and bonkers striker Faustino Asprilla. But, having lost their opening group games against Romania and the USA, Colombia found themselves in the unwanted position of having to beat Switzer-land *and* rely on a string of favourable results elsewhere. The Swiss were much better off – they were unbeaten and were likely to qualify whatever this result. They boasted the danger-ous attacking trio of Stephane Chapuisat, Adrian Knup, and Alain Sutter, and were UFWC champions on account of thrash-ing Romania 4-1 in the previous game. With California embrac-ing the celebration of the beautiful game, 81,000 spectators crammed into the Stanford Stadium in Palo Alto, south of San Francisco. And Colombia, desperate to qualify, provided plenty of entertainment. Driven forward by Valderrama and Rincon, the Colombians were only kept at bay by some brilliant saves from Swiss keeper Marco Pascolo. Colombia finally beat Pascolo in the last minute of the first half, as Luis Herrera's free kick was headed home by Herman Gaviria. In the second half Swit-zerland seemed to be content to keep the score down, sitting back and creating few chances for their talented forwards.

Colombia made sure of the points in the final minute, through Harold Lozano. But the victory wasn't enough for Colombia, who failed to qualify. The team returned home in disgrace, with one Colombian newspaper offering the headline: 'Humiliated!' Singled out for individual criticism was 27-year-old defender Andres Escobar, who inadvertently scored an own goal in the loss to the USA. On 2 July, Escobar was sitting in a car outside a Medellin nightclub when he was approached by an angry gang and shot six times at point blank range. The gunman, mob bodyguard Humberto Munez, apparently shouted, 'Own goal! Own goal!' as he murdered the footballer. Escobar's death shocked Colombia and the world. Munez was arrested and sentenced to 43 years in jail, but served only 11, being controversially released in 2005. While the World Cup continued in the USA, football in Colombia was put on hold. It would be more than six months until Colombia would defend their UFWC title – losing out to South Korea. Russia subsequently took the title to Euro 96.

HALL OF FAME - ANDRES ESCOBAR

Tragic defender **Andres Escobar** was known to fans as El Caballero del Futbol, or the Gentleman of Football. Born in 1967, Escobar scored a diving header against Peter Shilton and England at Wembley in 1988, and went on to play in two World Cups. But his most infamous strike was the catastrophic deflected own goal against the USA at the 1994 tournament. Escobar slid to intercept a John Harkes cross, but inadvertently directed the ball into his own net. Colombia lost 2-1 and were eliminated from the World Cup. Upon his return to Colombia, aged 27, Escobar was shot dead – executed for scoring football's most famous own goal.

MATCH # 674

Czech Republic 1-2 Germany AET
30 June 1996

European Championships final
Wembley Stadium, London, England
Scorers: Berger (Czech Republic),
Bierhoff (2) (Germany)

Euro 96, the 10th European Championships tournament, is remembered in its host country as a *Three Lions*-singing, face-painting, flag-waving, penalty-missing rollercoaster ride. Germany knocked England out at the semi-final stage on penalties, with Gareth Southgate missing the vital decisive spot kick. UFWC champs the Czech Republic also reached the final via a penalty shoot-out, at the expense of France. Although the German side contained more household names, the Czech team had won much respect. Germany could call upon established players like Thomas Hassler, Matthias Sammer, Stefan Kuntz, and Jurgen Klinsmann, but the Czech Republic had rising stars such as Pavel Nedved, Karel Poborsky, Patrick Berger, and Vladimir Smicer. After their strong showing in this tournament, brilliant playmaker Nedved would go on to great things at Juventus, Poborsky would sign for Manchester United, and Berger and Smicer would end up at Liverpool. Smicer flew home two days before the final to get married, but returned to take a place on the substitutes' bench. Among the rule changes implemented for Euro 96 was the introduction of the Golden Goal – a goal scored during extra-time that would immediately win the match. The rule change would prove decisive. Germany were first to bare their teeth in this encounter, with Kuntz and Klinsmann both coming close to opening the score. But the

Czech Republic also created chances, mostly through the clever running of Poborsky and Berger. There was no score at half-time, but 15 minutes into the second half Poborsky surged towards the penalty area and flew theatrically over Sammer's outstretched leg. The Germans claimed that the challenge had been a fair one *and* that it was outside the penalty area. Nevertheless, Italian referee Pierluigi Pairetto awarded a penalty. Berger converted with his left foot, and the Czechs had the advantage. A wounded Germany pushed for an equaliser but struggled to find it. Then, with 13 minutes left to play, manager Berti Vogts brought on Oliver Bierhoff. The Udinese striker duly scored with his first touch, nodding in Christian Ziege's free kick. Both sides pressed for a winner, but the 90 minutes ended with the scores level. The game went into extra-time. Both sides must have been contemplating another penalty shoot-out, but Bierhoff had other ideas. Five minutes into the extra period, the super sub received the ball with his back to goal, spun his marker, and fired a left foot shot past Czech keeper Petr Kouba. Again there was controversy – an offside flag was raised. But the referee decided that the offside player was not interfering with play. Bierhoff's goal stood, and it was a Golden Goal. The final whistle blew, and Germany could celebrate. Skipper Klinsmann received the Euro trophy from the Queen, although she neglected to hand over the intangible UFWC prize. Nevertheless, Germany were UFWC champions, and they would hold the title for almost two years, losing out to Brazil in 1998.

MATCH # 701

Brazil 0-3 France
13 July 1998
World Cup final
Stade de France, Saint-Denis, France
Scorers: Zidane (2), Petit (France)

The greatest night in the history of French football began with confusion and controversy. Brazil's official team sheet showed that mercurial striker Ronaldo, already the scorer of four goals in the tournament, had been replaced in the line up by Edmundo. Brazil fans and neutrals were united in disappointment, believing they had been robbed of a chance to see perhaps the world's best player on the world's best stage. Rumours circulated that Ronaldo was injured, had been taken to hospital, and had not travelled to the game. Then, in a remarkable turnaround, Brazilian officials issued a new team sheet, with Ronaldo restored to the line up, and his name marked in large capital letters. Further rumours suggested that powerful unknowns, be they governing bodies or sponsors, had demanded Ronaldo play, whatever his state of fitness. The unfortunate Edmundo, nicknamed 'The Animal', was understandably unhappy, and was said to have been at the centre of a rather heated debate in the Brazilian dressing room. It was later reported that Ronaldo had suffered a convulsive fit just hours before the game, apparently as a result of emotional stress. Whatever the truth, the Brazil team took to the field for this World Cup / UFWC double-header holding hands but apparently in disarray. The stadium PA system played the theme from *Star Wars*, highly appropriate if Brazil's big names were at loggerheads. Even the most causal observer could see that something was awry. Ronaldo was clearly unfit, a shadow of himself, and barely able to touch the ball. Talented individuals like Roberto Carlos, Rivaldo, and Bebeto should still have given France a good game. But the French also had excellent players, including Marcel Desailly, Didier Deschamps, and Zinedine Zidane. And the night that was supposed to belong to Ronaldo ended up belonging to Zidane. Despite being seen to vomit on the pitch, 'Zizou' scored twice in the first half, heading home corner kicks from both flanks. By way of response Brazil rarely threatened, although French keeper Fabian Barthez looked characteristically shaky, and almost dropped a couple of crosses into his own net. Desailly was sent off in the second half, but Brazil were unable to turn their man advantage into goals. Indeed, with Brazil foraging up front, substitute Patrick Viera sent fellow Arsenal midfielder Emmanuel Petit through to score a third killer goal in injury time. At the final whistle Brazilian players and fans were reduced to tears. Such a comprehensive defeat was hard for them to bear. But there was joy for France, with Deschamps becoming the first French captain to lift the World Cup. Zidane, despite having been sent-off in the first round, emerged as the star of the tournament, and a national hero. He had, within the space of 90 minutes, arguably eclipsed even the amazing achievements of the great Michel Platini. The French partied into the night, with over a million revellers packing the Champs Elysees in Paris. Who knows how many more might have turned up if they had known that they had also won the UFWC? Les Bleus held on to the unofficial title for nine games, before being dispossessed by Russia.

MATCH # 716

Israel 4-1 Russia
23 February 2000
Friendly
Kiryat-Eliezer Stadium, Haifa, Israel
Scorers: Badir (2), Udi, Nimni (Israel)
Beschastnykh (Russia)

The history of football in Israel is almost as complicated and confusing as the history of Israel itself. The Israel Football Association was formed in 1928, 20 years before the state of Israel even existed. For many years of no fixed abode, Israel have played under the governance of five of the six continental bodies, in Africa, Asia, Europe, Oceania, and South America. They actually won the Asian Nations Cup in 1964, before eventually joining UEFA in 1994. Israel had made three previous attempts to take the UFWC title, in 1969, 1990, and 1997, losing out to Sweden, Greece, and Germany respectively. By contrast, Russia had already won 40 UFWC title matches (23 as the USSR). The run-up to this game saw Israel (unassuming nickname: The Holy 11) in something approaching despair after an 8-0 aggregate stuffing by Denmark in the European Championships play-offs. But the Israelis learnt from their defeat. Appreciating that the Danes seemed to know something or other about the game of football, the Israel Football Association hired Danish coach Richard Moeller Nielsen. His Israeli side boasted two Premiership midfielders in Walid Badir and Avi Nimni. Badir was a Wimbledon player, and Nimni was coming to the end of a short stay at Derby County. Another Israeli midfielder, Idan Tal, would sign for Everton for in the months that followed this game, although his two-year stay at

Goodison Park was notable only for being extremely unnotable. Russia also lined up with a handful of familiar names. Alexei Smertin was at Locomotiv Moscow, although he would later play for Chelsea, Portsmouth, and Charlton. Up front were Zenit St Petersburg's Alexander Panov, soon to make a big money move to St Etienne, and Spartak Moscow striker Igor Titov, a great goalscorer unfortunately better known for failing a drugs test after a Euro 2004 play-off against Wales. The game began with Israel in the ascendancy. Badir headed the first goal after just three minutes, debutant Kfir Udi walked in the second after a defensive mix-up, and Badir drove in the third when a misplaced clearance fell at his feet. 3-0 down at half-time, Russia replaced Panov with their highest post-USSR goalscorer Vladimir Beschastnykh. The move appeared to pay dividends, as Beschastnykh converted a penalty in the 58th minute. Russia netted again and seemed to be back in the game – only for the goal to be ruled offside. Then Nimni scored a deflected shot for Israel to seal the 4-1 victory. The Russian press hammered their team, and manager Oleg Romantsev was said to be close to quitting. 'We are all to blame,' said Russian assistant coach Mikhail Gershkovich. 'We were very bad.' Accordingly, that meant Israel weren't particularly good, and, having held off Georgia in a 1-1 draw, the Israelis duly lost the UFWC title to the Czech Republic in April 2000 via a 4-1 reversal. However, the achievement of Israel cannot be overlooked, and they remain one of the unlikeliest sides ever to win the UFWC.

Alan Shearer, the last England captain to win the UFWC title

MATCH # 722

England 1-0 Germany
17 June 2000
European Championships
Stad du Pays, Charleroi, Belgium
Scorer: Shearer (England)

How the mighty had fallen. Previously regarded as the greatest team in the world, by 2000 England had not held the UFWC title for a full quarter of a century. England's 1975 title victory came, like the one in 1966, against Germany. It seemed that the two sides were indelibly linked as ultimate UFWC rivals. In June 2000 Germany were the reigning UFWC champions, having taken the title from the Czech Republic earlier in the month. And struggling England were unfavoured in the Euro group match, having lost their opening match of the tournament to Portugal, with skipper Alan Shearer in particular taking a barracking from the press. 'Fans want Owen not Shearer,' read one headline, with the article stating, 'Most England fans believe captain Alan Shearer should be left out of Kevin Keegan's starting line-up for Euro 2000, according to a new poll.' In the event, Keegan selected both Shearer and Michael Owen, alongside the likes of David Seaman, David Beckham, and Paul Scholes. Meanwhile, things were less than rosy in the German camp, with some pundits calling the side the worst in living memory. Coach Erich Ribbeck had been recalled from retirement on the golf courses of Tenerife just before the tournament began. Having stashed away his irons, he was able to call up stars like Oliver Kahn, Michael Ballack, and Carsten Jancker, but record goalscorer Oliver Bierhoff was unavailable, and in Lothar Mattaus Germany had a sweeper old enough to be Michael Owen's father. The match was one of few chances, although England edged things through the build-up play of Scholes and Beckham. The goal that settled matters came 53 minutes in. Beckham's free kick from the right was flicked on at the near post by a combination of Owen and a German defender. Shearer launched himself at the deflection and expertly headed home. Keegan said afterwards of his goalscorer and man of the match, 'He's answered his critics again. I just think he's the best at what he does and he's done it again tonight.' England won the group match and, even more excitingly, the Unofficial Football World Championships. Unfortunately, as is the case with a title that exists only on paper, there was no trophy for Shearer to hold aloft in Bobby Moore-style. 'England's ageing hero feasted mightily on his moment of glory by devouring his doubters,' reported *The Times*, calling the result, 'a famous victory secured by a leader who has had more stick than the PM at Question Time.' Thousands of jubilant England fans sang and danced and jumped into Charleroi's classical fountains, while others, regrettably, fought running battles with police. England surrendered the UFWC title to Romania three days later in a 3-2 defeat. Sick of his critics, Shearer quit international football following the Euro tournament. Keegan followed Shearer out of the door two games later following a World Cup qualifier defeat to, inevitably, Germany.

HALL OF FAME - ALAN SHEARER

Alan Shearer OBE scored 30 goals in 63 appearances for England. He scored on his international debut, and captained his country from 1996 to 2000. Born in Newcastle in 1970, he began his club career at Southampton, before moving to Blackburn Rovers, where he won the Premier League in 1995. Shearer signed for his hometown team Newcastle United in 1996, and became the club's all-time record goalscorer, as well as the top scorer in the history of the English Premiership, before retiring in 2006. Named by his own club chairman as a 'Mary Poppins figure', Shearer has nevertheless been involved in his fair share of scrapes. In 1997, during a club jolly in Dublin, Shearer gave Newcastle teammate Keith Gillespie a 'good hiding' for flicking bottle tops at him, leaving the Northern Ireland international bloodied in a gutter. 'It was all just high spirits,' explained Gillespie.

ENGLAND – INDISPUTABLY SECOND BEST

Despite maintaining consistent high regard in international football, England have rarely succeeded in tournament play. The nation's greatest moment came at Wembley in 1966, when Bobby Moore led his side to a World Cup / UFWC double. For a short while England were official and unofficial – and undisputed – world champions. That was the only time England won the official title, but the Three Lions have fared much better in the unofficial contest. Due partly to the British nations' dominance of early football, England have won more UFWC title matches than any other side – bar one. For England are second in the overall UFWC rankings – beneath the Auld Enemy. But a run of UFWC wins could see England challenge for the top spot, and re-ignite a fiery rivalry.

MATCH # 726

Italy 1-2 France AET
3 July 2000
European Championships final
Feyenoord Stadium, Rotterdam, Netherlands
Scorers: Wiltord, Trezeguet (France),
Delvecchio (Italy)

Italy beat Romania in the quarter-finals to take the UFWC title, and then defeated hosts the Netherlands in the semis to reach the final of Euro 2000. France beat Portugal courtesy of a Zinedine Zidane Golden Goal in their semi-final. The French were World Cup champions, and were confident that they were still the best team in the world. They had added Arsenal pair Patrick Viera and Thierry Henry plus AS Monaco's David Trezeguet to their starting 11 since the World Cup win. But their star player remained Zinedine Zidane, and the Juventus midfielder knew more than most that the Italian players he came up against every week would be no pushovers. Like all good Italian sides, this one was built from the back, with a solid back three of Fabio Cannavaro, Alessandro Nesta, and Mark Iuliano protecting big keeper Francesco Toldo. And, although the pacy French did most of the early running, the Italian rearguard held firm. Similarly, the French back four of Lilian Thuram, Laurent Blanc, Marcel Desailly, and Bixente Lizarazu – a quartet that had never finished on the losing side in 25 games together – seemed impenetrable. Few should have been surprised that the first half ended 0-0. But the deadlock was eventually broken in the 56th minute. Somewhat against the run of play, it was Italy who took the lead through the left foot of Marco Delvecchio. A goal to the good, and with a formidable defensive record, Italy proceeded to shut up shop. And they remained resolute until the very last minute. Then, with impeccable timing, French substitute Sylvain Wiltord squeezed into a rare gap and struck a left foot shot to bag a last-gasp equaliser. The French were jubilant, and the Italians were deflated. Going into Golden Goal extra-time the balance of play shifted significantly in favour of the French. Eight minutes into the extra period Trezeguet whacked a Robert Pires cross into the roof of the Italian net. Golden Goal, game over. It was a thrilling comeback, although a real slap in the face for the Italians. French coach Roger Lemerre described the result as 'a miracle'. France became the first reigning World Cup champions to win the European Championships. They also won the UFWC, and held it for eight months before being dispossessed by Spain.

HALL OF FAME - ZINEDINE ZIDANE

Zinedine Zidane eclipsed even the great Michel Platini with his World Cup / UFWC winning performance in 1998. 'Zizou', a Frenchman of Algerian descent, was born in Marseille in 1972. Stoop-shouldered, with a famous bald spot, Zidane is a rather unlikely but much-loved hero. The magical midfielder retired from international football in 2004, but quickly returned to the French team in 2005 to help them qualify for the 2006 World Cup. A star at club level, Zidane has won the European Supercup and Serie A with Juventus and the Champions League and La Liga with Real Madrid. He was named European Footballer of the Year in 1998, and FIFA World Footballer of the Year in 1998, 2000, and 2003.

MATCH # 754

Czech Republic 3-1 Netherlands
10 September 2003

European Championships qualifier
Toyota Arena, Prague, Czech Republic
Scorers: Koller, Poborsky, Baros (Czech Republic)
Van der Vaart (Netherlands)

The Netherlands took the UFWC title from Spain in March 2002 and remained unbeaten for 12 matches, winning 10 and drawing three. The Dutch side was full of household names, with Edwin Van der Saar in goal, Michael Reiziger and Jaap Stam at the back, Marc Overmars and Edgar Davids in midfield, and a front pairing of Patrick Kluivert and Ruud van Nistlerooy. The Netherlands failed to qualify for the 2002 World Cup, and as a result the UFWC title had not been contested at Japan and Korea. Now the Dutch were seeking to qualify for the 2004 European Championships, and they were running neck and neck with the Czech Republic. The two sides were level on points at the top of qualifying group C, but this UFWC title match would shatter the parity. The preceding qualifying match between the two sides in Rotterdam ended as a 1-1 stalemate. The return fixture in Prague would be much more interesting. The Czech Republic were unbeaten in 15 games, and the side that first shone at Euro 96 had very much come of age. Pavel Nedved, Vladimir Smicer, and Karel Poborsky were all veterans of the Euro 96 campaign, and they were joined in the side by Petr Cech, Jan Koller, Tomas Rosicky, and Milan Baros. The game began disastrously for the Dutch. Just 14 minutes in Davids fouled Poborsky in the area and was sent off. Koller rattled in the resultant penalty to give the Czechs the lead.

Seven minutes before half-time that lead was doubled as Nedved sent through Poborsky, who chipped Van der Saar. The Czechs continued to exploit their man advantage in the second half, but the Dutch made things interestingly when Rafael Van der Vaart's shot was inadvertently deflected into Petr Cech's net by Martin Jiranek. The revitalised Netherlands pushed forward in search of an equaliser, but it was not to come. In injury time, Liverpool's Baros rounded Van der Saar to kill the game. The Czechs topped the group, but both sides ended up qualifying for Euro 2004. But the Czech Republic could not take the UFWC title into that tournament – they lost it to the Republic of Ireland.

HALL OF FAME - KAREL POBORSKY

Karel Poborsky, sometimes spelled Poborski, is his fledgling country's most-capped footballer. The attacking midfielder played in the Czech Republic's first ever match in 1994, and subsequently made over 100 appearances for the side. He represented the Czech Republic at three European Championships finals, in 1996, 2000, and 2004, and helped his country qualify for the 2006 World Cup finals. At club level, Poborsky spent two seasons at Manchester United before playing for Benfica, Lazio, and Sparta Prague. Born in 1972, Poborsky is nicknamed 'Steve' after Canadian skier Steve Podborski. In his early career he sported several stereotypically bad 'footballer's haircuts', from straggly rock perm to curly mullet, and it was noted that his form improved noticeably following his decision to go with a short back and sides.

MATCH # 761

Republic of Ireland 0-3 Nigeria
29 May 2004
Friendly

The Valley, London

Scorers: Ogbeche, Martins (2) (Nigeria)

Algeria, Cameroon, Egypt, the Ivory Coast, Morocco, South Africa, and Tunisia had already tried and failed. Now it was Nigeria's chance to become the first African nation to win the UFWC. The Super Eagles had tried once before, in 1994, but lost out to Romania. Now the UFWC came to Charlton Athletic's The Valley. Why the unusual choice of venue? This friendly match was part of a three-team tournament called the Unity Cup, played in London between nations that had large communities in the city. Who said the UFWC was the only international football tournament that nobody had ever heard of? Ireland, Nigeria, and Jamaica were the unlikely competitors. But, in its inaugural fixture, the Unity Cup was hit by something of a scandal. Nigeria arrived for the tournament without their two biggest stars, Nwankwo Kanu and captain Jay-Jay Okocha. The pair had been criticised earlier in the year by Nigerian sports and social development minister Colonel Musa Mohammed for delaying their arrival at the African Cup of Nations Tournament. 'This has no doubt affected the level of readiness of the team,' said the Colonel. The pair didn't turn up at all for the Unity Cup, prompting Nigeria Football Authority chief Taiwo Ogunjobi to cry foul. He claimed that Okocha was being encouraged to lead his country's star players to boycott the tournament. 'I am beginning to believe some people are working against the ambition of the star player to rule the continent as the African footballer of the year,' said Ogunjobi. In the absence of bigger names, Nigeria handed a debut to highly-rated teenager Obafemi Martins. The 19-year-old Inter Milan striker didn't disappoint. Ireland, resting the likes of Roy Keane and Shay Given in anticipation of World Cup qualifiers, were thoroughly outclassed by a lively Nigeria. Bartholemew Ogbeche opened the scoring in the first half, and young Martins added a second four minutes after the break. Ogbeche made it three with 30 minutes to play, and the game was well and truly settled. 'Any time Nigeria call on me I will make myself available,' said impressive debutant Martins. Nigeria did call on Martins for subsequent matches, although Okocha missed out due to tiredness and 'travel difficulties'. In the Unity Cup, Nigeria beat Jamaica 2-0 to win the 2004 Unity Cup. A four-team 2005 tournament was delayed indefinitely due to policing difficulties. As for the UFWC, Nigeria became the first African side to win the title, 43 years after Morocco became the first African side to contest it in 1961.

HALL OF FAME - OBAFEMI MARTINS

Teenage UFWC goal hero **Obafemi Martins** made his international debut for Nigeria in this 2004 UFWC match despite being previously named in an international squad by Cameroon. Martins didn't turn up for that match. 'It is not true that I am from Cameroon,' he explained. 'I am a Nigerian, and I remain loyal to my country.' Martins was born in Lagos in 1984, and made his name at club level with Inter Milan. Noted for his pace, Martins has run the 100-metre sprint in less than 11 seconds.

MATCH # 772

Zimbabwe 2-0 Angola
27 March 2005
World Cup qualifier
Harare, Zimbabwe
Scorers: Kawondera, Mwaruwaru (Zimbabwe)

This World Cup qualifier doubled as an African Nations Cup qualifier, and trebled as a UFWC title match. The unlikely UFWC champs were Angola, a Southern African country perhaps better known for its long-running civil war than for its footballing prowess. But the Palancas Negras, or Black Impalas, were racing up the UFWC rankings table on merit having taken the title from Nigeria in a World Cup qualifier in June 2004 and remaining unbeaten for eight games. Angola's star man was Benfica's Pedro Mantorras. Zimbabwe's recent sporting history had been somewhat overshadowed by political and social strife under the government of President Robert Mugabe. A keen football fan, Mugabe entrusted the administration of the national side to his nephew Leo. But Leo was ousted from the post after a £35,000 grant from FIFA to develop youth football was curiously misplaced. Uncle Robert then handed control to information minister Jonathan Moyo, who saw the national team as a propaganda opportunity. Seeking to cheer up a downtrodden population, Moyo dedicated money to improving the side, and personally penned uplifting lyrics for a musical television advert: *'We are on the hunting grounds. We are going for goals, goals, goals. Score Warriors. Go, go, Warriors.'* Undeniably catchy. Suitably inspired, the Warriors became something of a force on the football field. Dreadlocked coach Charles Mhlauri's key man was ageing skipper Peter Ndlovu, playing out his time in South Africa after spending most of his career in England. Ndlovu spurned the best chance of the tight first half, driving a shot wide from close range. Zimbabwe brought on Shingirai Kawondera at half-time, and the striker quickly opened the scoring with a drilled shot from the edge of the box. Zimbabwe sealed the win in front of 45,000 delighted fans through a Benjamin Mwaruwaru header. New UFWC champs Zimbabwe remained unbeaten for nine games, winning the 2005 COSAFA Cup in the process. Robert Mugabe rewarded his players with plots of freshly-razed land, much to the consternation of the now-homeless former residents. Zimbabwe qualified for the African Nations Cup, but failed to qualify for the World Cup. The Warriors finished third in their group, behind the side they won the UFWC title from – the Black Impalas of Angola – and the side they would eventually lose the title to – the Super Eagles of Nigeria.

HALL OF FAME - PETER NDLOVU

Warriors captain **Peter Ndlovu** was Zimbabwe's all-time leading goalscorer when he retired from international football in 2006. Highly regarded as the talisman of his team, Ndlovu has nevertheless been caught up in his fair share of controversies, mostly involving women, including a 'seductive fraudster' named Alice Miya. 'I meet a lot of people, and many people come to my house and I can't know all of them,' Ndlovu told *New Zimbabwe*. Born in Bulawayo in 1973, 'Nuddy' played at club level in England with Coventry City, Birmingham City, and Sheffield United, before signing for South Africa's Mamelodi Sundowns.

MATCH # 782

Romania 3-0 Nigeria
16 November 2005
Friendly

Bucharest

Nicolae, Petre, Rosu (Romania)

For reasons that no one seemed to be able to properly explain, rather than playing the Democratic Republic of Congo at home as fixtured, Nigeria travelled away to play Romania in a hastily rearranged friendly. Few people seemed to know about the match – only 800 spectators turned up. And the confusion didn't stop there. The Super Eagles arrived in Bucharest four hours before kick-off, with just six players and no manager. There was no sign of key players like Jay Jay Okocha, Nwankwo Kanu, Joseph Yobo, Obafemi Martins, and Aiyegbeni Yakubu, who had variously missed previous matches dues to conflicts with the Nigerian Football Authority (NFA). This time, the NFA's late issuing of invitations for the last-minute match was also partly to blame. In some cases players were given only 48 hours notice, with clubs requiring seven days notice to release players for international duty. Manager Austin Eguavoen didn't turn up either. 'The game was arranged, called off, and suddenly it was given the seal of certainty, by which time I was unable to report because of other assignments,' he told the *Daily Independent*. In Eguavoen's absence, former Everton striker Daniel Amokachi took charge of the team, and the situation. He arranged for the match to be delayed by two hours – forcing Romanian TV to abandon plans to televise the match – and then dashed to the Nigerian embassy to mount a desperate last-ditch search around Romania for players with Nigerian passports. He then procured a set of shirts – the Super Eagles had also forgotten to bring their kits. With 10 minutes to go until kick-off, the Nigerians were yet to emerge for their warm-up – in freezing cold conditions. 'We were even thinking the game might not happen,' Romanian defender Razvan Rat told the *Bucharest Daily News*. But the game did eventually get under way – a further 20 minutes late – with Amokachi having managed to increase his makeshift squad to 12. Romania may have lined up without star players Adrian Mutu and Christian Chivu, but Nigeria lined up without any recognised players whatsoever. 'I don't even know the names of the players we played against,' admitted Rat. One of the Nigerian players Rat failed to recognise was debutant Sam Sodje of Brentford, who picked up an injury during the game but was forced to play on due to the lack of substitutes. It should come as no surprise to learn that Nigeria were duly stuffed 3-0, with Daniel Nicolae, Floretin Petre, and Laurentiu Rosu the goalscorers for new champions Romania. 'Anybody who expects that we should have won that match is merely deluding himself,' explained missing manager Eguavoen, 'because you can't arrive for a match four hours to the game and expect to win.' Nigeria were thoroughly deserved losers. The UFWC title returned to Europe for the first time in 18 months. The last time Romania won the UFWC, in 2000, they held the title for just four days. This time they managed to defeat Armenia and Slovakia, but then lost 2-0 to Uruguay in May 2006. Uruguay held off Serbia, Libya and Tunisia in the run-up to the 2006 World Cup. But the South Americans had failed to qualify for the tournament, so the UFWC title was not contested at Germany 2006, and Uruguay remained Unofficial Football World Champions.

COMPLETE RESULTS

KEY

Featured CLASSIC MATCHES highlighted in **BOLD**.

AET = After extra-time. PEN = After penalties. * = Won on penalties. A-A = Match abandoned. BH = British Home Championships / Home Internationals. CA = Copa America / South American Championships. CC = CONCACAF Championships. CO = COSAFA Nations Cup. EC = European Championships. EQ = European Championships qualifier. FR = Friendly fixture. PA = Pan American Championships. WC = World Cup. WQ = World Cup qualifier.

1	30/11/1872	SCOTLAND 0-0 ENGLAND	Glasgow	FR
2	08/03/1873	ENGLAND 4-2 SCOTLAND	London	FR
3	07/03/1874	SCOTLAND 2-1 ENGLAND	Glasgow	FR
4	06/03/1875	ENGLAND 2-2 SCOTLAND	London	FR
5	04/03/1876	SCOTLAND 3-0 ENGLAND	Glasgow	FR
6	25/03/1876	SCOTLAND 4-0 WALES	Glasgow	FR
7	03/03/1877	ENGLAND 1-3 SCOTLAND	London	FR
8	05/03/1877	WALES 0-2 SCOTLAND	Wrexham	FR
9	02/03/1878	SCOTLAND 7-2 ENGLAND	Glasgow	FR
10	23/03/1878	SCOTLAND 9-0 WALES	Glasgow	FR
11	05/04/1879	ENGLAND 5-4 SCOTLAND	London	FR
12	13/03/1880	SCOTLAND 5-4 ENGLAND	Glasgow	FR

HALL OF FAME – SEGAR BASTARD

Segar Richard Bastard not only played for England, winning his only cap in a 1880 UFWC loss to Scotland, but he also refereed two England matches. This genuine Bastard in the black also refereed the 1878 FA Cup Final. Born in Bow in 1854, Bastard played club football for Upton Park FC and was also a top-class cricketer and a renowned gambler – he was one of the first footballers to own a racehorse.

13	27/03/1880	SCOTLAND 5-1 WALES	Glasgow	FR
14	12/03/1881	ENGLAND 1-6 SCOTLAND	London	FR

| 15 | 14/03/1881 | WALES 1-5 SCOTLAND | Wrexham | FR |
| 16 | 11/03/1882 | SCOTLAND 5-1 ENGLAND | Glasgow | FR |

HALL OF FAME – ANDREW WATSON

Scotland defender **Andrew Watson** was the very first black international footballer. Born in British Guiana in 1857, the scholarly Watson studied philosophy and mathematics at Glasgow University before finding fame on the football field with Queen's Park FC. Watson played three games for Scotland in 1881 and 1882 – all UFWC victories. Records from the time make no note of Watson's skin colour, although they do report that he wore brown boots rather than more common black ones.

17	25/03/1882	SCOTLAND 5-0 WALES	Glasgow	FR
18	10/03/1883	ENGLAND 2-3 SCOTLAND	Sheffield	FR
19	12/03/1883	WALES 0-3 SCOTLAND	Wrexham	FR

THE BRITISH HOME CHAMPIONSHIP

The world's first international football tournament formalised friendly matches between England, Ireland, Scotland, and Wales. The format varied, as did the name, and the BHC never attained great prestige, but the tournament continued in one form or another for a full 101 years before being scrapped due to hooliganism and a growing lack of interest.

20	**26/01/1884**	**IRELAND 0-5 SCOTLAND**	**Belfast**	**BH**
21	15/03/1884	SCOTLAND 1-0 ENGLAND	Glasgow	BH
22	29/03/1884	SCOTLAND 4-1 WALES	Glasgow	BH

23	14/03/1885	SCOTLAND 8-2 IRELAND	Glasgow	BH
24	21/03/1885	ENGLAND 1-1 SCOTLAND	London	BH
25	23/03/1885	WALES 1-8 SCOTLAND	Wrexham	BH
26	20/03/1886	IRELAND 2-7 SCOTLAND	Belfast	BH
27	31/03/1886	SCOTLAND 1-1 ENGLAND	Glasgow	BH
28	10/04/1886	SCOTLAND 4-1 WALES	Glasgow	BH

THE IFAB

Formed in 1886 by the Football Associations of England, Ireland, Scotland, and Wales, the International Football Association Board was created to determine consistent rules for international football, a role it continues to fulfil to this day. Initial IFAB rules were rudimentary – a 19th century goalie, for example, could handle the ball anywhere on the pitch.

29	19/02/1887	SCOTLAND 4-1 IRELAND	Glasgow	BH
30	19/03/1887	ENGLAND 2-3 SCOTLAND	Blackburn	BH
31	21/03/1887	WALES 0-2 SCOTLAND	Wrexham	BH
32	10/03/1888	SCOTLAND 5-1 WALES	Edinburgh	BH
33	17/03/1888	SCOTLAND 0-5 ENGLAND	Glasgow	BH
34	31/03/1888	IRELAND 1-5 ENGLAND	Belfast	BH
35	23/02/1889	ENGLAND 4-1 WALES	Stoke	BH
36	02/03/1889	ENGLAND 6-1 IRELAND	Liverpool	BH

37	13/04/1889	ENGLAND 2-3 SCOTLAND	London	BH
38	15/04/1889	WALES 0-0 SCOTLAND	Wrexham	BH
39	22/03/1890	SCOTLAND 5-0 WALES	Paisley	BH
40	29/03/1890	IRELAND 1-4 SCOTLAND	Belfast	BH
41	05/04/1890	SCOTLAND 1-1 ENGLAND	Glasgow	BH
42	07/03/1891	ENGLAND 4-1 WALES	Sunderland	BH
43	21/03/1891	WALES 3-4 SCOTLAND	Wrexham	BH
44	28/03/1891	SCOTLAND 2-1 IRELAND	Glasgow	BH
45	06/04/1891	ENGLAND 2-1 SCOTLAND	Blackburn	BH
46	05/03/1892	WALES 0-2 ENGLAND	Wrexham	BH
47	05/03/1892	IRELAND 0-2 ENGLAND	Belfast	BH
48	02/04/1892	SCOTLAND 1-4 ENGLAND	Glasgow	BH
49	25/02/1893	ENGLAND 6-1 IRELAND	Birmingham	BH
50	13/03/1893	ENGLAND 6-0 WALES	Stoke	BH
51	01/04/1893	ENGLAND 5-2 SCOTLAND	London	BH
52	03/03/1894	IRELAND 2-2 ENGLAND	Belfast	BH
53	12/03/1894	WALES 1-5 ENGLAND	Wrexham	BH
54	07/04/1894	SCOTLAND 2-2 ENGLAND	Glasgow	BH
55	**09/03/1895**	**ENGLAND 9-0 IRELAND**	**Derby**	**BH**
56	18/03/1895	ENGLAND 1-1 WALES	London	BH

57	06/04/1895	ENGLAND 3-0 SCOTLAND	Liverpool	BH
58	07/03/1896	IRELAND 0-2 ENGLAND	Belfast	BH
59	16/03/1896	WALES 1-9 ENGLAND	Cardiff	BH
60	04/04/1896	SCOTLAND 2-1 ENGLAND	Glasgow	BH
61	20/03/1897	WALES 2-2 SCOTLAND	Wrexham	BH
62	27/03/1897	SCOTLAND 5-1 IRELAND	Glasgow	BH
63	03/04/1897	ENGLAND 1-2 SCOTLAND	London	BH
64	19/03/1898	SCOTLAND 5-2 WALES	Motherwell	BH
65	26/03/1898	IRELAND 0-3 SCOTLAND	Belfast	BH
66	02/04/1898	SCOTLAND 1-3 ENGLAND	Glasgow	BH
67	**18/02/1899**	**ENGLAND 13-2 IRELAND**	**Sunderland**	**BH**
68	20/03/1899	ENGLAND 4-0 WALES	Bristol	BH
69	08/04/1899	ENGLAND 2-1 SCOTLAND	Birmingham	BH
70	17/03/1900	IRELAND 0-2 ENGLAND	Dublin	BH
71	26/03/1900	WALES 1-1 ENGLAND	Cardiff	BH
72	07/04/1900	SCOTLAND 4-1 ENGLAND	Glasgow	BH

THE 1900 OLYMPIC GAMES

The Paris Olympics saw the first 'organised' international football competition, as sides representing France, Great Britain, and Belgium played exhibition matches, but no medals were awarded, and none of the results stand in official records.

73	23/02/1901	SCOTLAND 11-0 IRELAND	Glasgow	BH
74	02/03/1901	WALES 1-1 SCOTLAND	Wrexham	BH
75	30/03/1901	ENGLAND 2-2 SCOTLAND	London	BH
76	01/03/1902	IRELAND 1-5 SCOTLAND	Belfast	BH
77	15/03/1902	SCOTLAND 5-1 WALES	Greenock	BH
78	05/04/1902	SCOTLAND A-A ENGLAND	Glasgow	BH

THE IBROX DISASTER

Tragedy occurred at this 1902 UFWC match at Ibrox Park as a section of the West Stand collapsed. 'A portion of terracing, packed with a seething crowd of humanity, gave way under unwanted pressure,' reported *The Scotsman*. 'The spectators were precipitated to the ground from a height of around 40 or 50 feet.' 26 people were killed and more than 500 injured. The game was abandoned.

79	03/05/1902	ENGLAND 2-2 SCOTLAND	Birmingham	BH
80	09/03/1903	WALES 0-1 SCOTLAND	Cardiff	BH
81	21/03/1903	SCOTLAND 0-2 IRELAND	Glasgow	BH
82	28/03/1903	IRELAND 2-0 WALES	Belfast	BH
83	12/03/1904	IRELAND 1-3 ENGLAND	Belfast	BH
84	29/03/1904	WALES 2-2 ENGLAND	Wrexham	FR
85	09/04/1904	SCOTLAND 0-1 ENGLAND	Glasgow	BH

FIFA

The Fédération Internationale de Football Association was founded in Paris on 21 May 1904 as the official body to govern international football. The seven founding members were Belgium, Denmark, France, the Netherlands, Spain, Sweden and Switzerland.

86	25/02/1905	ENGLAND	1-1	IRELAND	Middlesbrough	BH
87	27/03/1905	ENGLAND	3-1	WALES	Liverpool	BH
88	01/04/1905	ENGLAND	1-0	SCOTLAND	London	BH
89	17/02/1906	IRELAND	0-5	ENGLAND	Belfast	BH
90	19/03/1906	WALES	0-1	ENGLAND	Cardiff	BH
91	07/04/1906	SCOTLAND	2-1	ENGLAND	Glasgow	BH
92	**04/03/1907**	**WALES**	**1-0**	**SCOTLAND**	**Wrexham**	**BH**
93	18/03/1907	ENGLAND	1-1	WALES	Fulham	BH
94	07/03/1908	SCOTLAND	2-1	WALES	Dundee	BH
95	14/03/1908	IRELAND	0-5	SCOTLAND	Dublin	BH
96	04/04/1908	SCOTLAND	1-1	ENGLAND	Glasgow	BH

THE 1908 OLYMPIC GAMES

Olympic football competitions were farcical up until this point, but in 1908 at the London Olympics a 'proper' football tournament saw a united Great Britain team beat out Denmark, the Netherlands, Sweden, and France. GB won football gold again in 1912. But both wins were overshadowed by arguments over the presence of professional players, and neither tournament could be realistically described as a success.

HALL OF FAME – VIVIAN WOODWARD

England skipper **Vivian John Woodward** was regarded as the best player of his generation, scoring 29 goals in 23 senior international appearances, and captaining the British amateur side to gold in the 1908 and 1912 Olympic Games. He scored 44 times in 30 games for the amateur side. Born in 1879, he scored Tottenham Hotspur's first goal in league football, and later played over 100 games for Chelsea. Regarded as football's great gentleman, Woodward made a point of shaking the hand of every opposition player before matches. Enlisted in 1914, Woodward survived the Great War, dying in 1954 aged 74.

97	01/03/1909	WALES 3-2 SCOTLAND	Wrexham	BH
98	15/03/1909	ENGLAND 2-0 WALES	Nottingham	BH
99	03/04/1909	ENGLAND 2-0 SCOTLAND	London	BH
100	**29/05/1909**	**HUNGARY 2-4 ENGLAND**	**Budapest**	**FR**

THE WORLD GAME

Much of Europe was now playing international football under the FIFA umbrella, and in 1909 Hungary became the first team from outside of the British Isles to contest the UFWC. In the same year, South Africa became the first non-European nation to join FIFA. Argentina and Chile joined from South America in 1912. Football was becoming a world game, but the strong British sides retained control of the UFWC.

101	31/05/1909	HUNGARY 2-8 ENGLAND	Budapest	FR
102	01/06/1909	AUSTRIA 1-8 ENGLAND	Vienna	FR

103	12/02/1910	IRELAND 1-1 ENGLAND	Belfast	BH
104	14/03/1910	WALES 0-1 ENGLAND	Cardiff	BH
105	02/04/1910	SCOTLAND 2-0 ENGLAND	Glasgow	BH
106	06/03/1911	WALES 2-2 SCOTLAND	Cardiff	BH
107	18/03/1911	SCOTLAND 2-0 IRELAND	Glasgow	BH
108	01/04/1911	ENGLAND 1-1 SCOTLAND	Liverpool	BH
109	02/03/1912	SCOTLAND 1-0 WALES	Edinburgh	BH
110	16/03/1912	IRELAND 1-4 SCOTLAND	Belfast	BH
111	23/03/1912	SCOTLAND 1-1 ENGLAND	Glasgow	BH
112	03/03/1913	WALES 0-0 SCOTLAND	Wrexham	BH
113	15/03/1913	IRELAND 1-2 SCOTLAND	Dublin	BH
114	05/04/1913	ENGLAND 1-0 SCOTLAND	London	BH
115	14/02/1914	ENGLAND 0-3 IRELAND	Middlesbrough	BH
116	14/03/1914	IRELAND 1-1 SCOTLAND	Belfast	BH

THE FIRST WORLD WAR

The Great War put an end to international football fixtures for five and a half years, and stole the lives of many of the era's best footballers. The only match of note played during the conflict was the historic Christmas Truce game between British and German soldiers in No Man's Land on 25 December 1914.

| 117 | 25/10/1919 | IRELAND 1-1 ENGLAND | Belfast | BH |

118	14/02/1920	IRELAND 2-2 WALES	Belfast	BH
119	13/03/1920	SCOTLAND 3-0 IRELAND	Glasgow	BH
120	10/04/1920	ENGLAND 5-4 SCOTLAND	Sheffield	BH
121	23/10/1920	ENGLAND 2-0 IRELAND	Sunderland	BH
122	14/03/1921	WALES 0-0 ENGLAND	Cardiff	BH
123	09/04/1921	SCOTLAND 3-0 ENGLAND	Glasgow	BH
124	04/02/1922	WALES 2-1 SCOTLAND	Wrexham	BH
125	13/03/1922	ENGLAND 1-0 WALES	Liverpool	BH
126	08/04/1922	ENGLAND 0-1 SCOTLAND	Birmingham	BH
127	**03/03/1923**	**N. IRELAND 0-1 SCOTLAND**	**Belfast**	**BH**
128	17/03/1923	SCOTLAND 2-0 WALES	Paisley	BH
129	14/04/1923	SCOTLAND 2-2 ENGLAND	Glasgow	BH
130	16/02/1924	WALES 2-0 SCOTLAND	Cardiff	BH
131	03/03/1924	ENGLAND 1-2 WALES	Blackburn	BH
132	15/03/1924	N. IRELAND 0-1 WALES	Belfast	BH

THE 1924 OLYMPIC GAMES

For the first time FIFA organised a successful football tournament, albeit exclusively for amateur players. 16 sides took part, but England, Northern Ireland, Scotland, and Wales all stayed away. 60,000 spectators watched Uruguay beat Switzerland in the final. The 1928 tournament was also won by Uruguay, and the successful events prompted FIFA to consider its own football championship.

133	14/02/1925	SCOTLAND	3-1	WALES	Edinburgh	BH
134	28/02/1925	N. IRELAND	0-3	SCOTLAND	Belfast	BH
135	04/04/1925	SCOTLAND	2-0	ENGLAND	Glasgow	BH
136	31/10/1925	WALES	0-3	SCOTLAND	Cardiff	BH
137	27/02/1926	SCOTLAND	4-0	N. IRELAND	Glasgow	BH
138	17/04/1926	ENGLAND	0-1	SCOTLAND	Manchester	BH
139	30/10/1926	SCOTLAND	3-0	WALES	Glasgow	BH
140	26/02/1927	N. IRELAND	0-2	SCOTLAND	Belfast	BH
141	02/04/1927	SCOTLAND	1-2	ENGLAND	Glasgow	BH
142	11/05/1927	BELGIUM	1-9	ENGLAND	Brussels	FR
143	21/05/1927	LUXEMBOURG	2-5	ENGLAND	Esch-sur-Alzette	FR
144	26/05/1927	FRANCE	0-6	ENGLAND	Colombes	FR
145	22/10/1927	N. IRELAND	2-0	ENGLAND	Belfast	BH
146	04/02/1928	N. IRELAND	1-2	WALES	Belfast	BH
147	27/10/1928	SCOTLAND	4-2	WALES	Glasgow	BH
148	23/02/1929	N. IRELAND	3-7	SCOTLAND	Belfast	BH
149	13/04/1929	SCOTLAND	1-0	ENGLAND	Glasgow	BH
150	26/05/1929	NORWAY	3-7	SCOTLAND	Bergen	FR
151	01/06/1929	GERMANY	1-1	SCOTLAND	Berlin	FR
152	04/06/1929	NETHERL.	0-2	SCOTLAND	Amsterdam	FR

153	26/10/1929	WALES 2-4 SCOTLAND	Cardiff	BH
154	22/02/1930	SCOTLAND 3-1 N. IRELAND	Glasgow	BH
155	**05/04/1930**	**ENGLAND 5-2 SCOTLAND**	**London**	**BH**
156	10/05/1930	GERMANY 3-3 ENGLAND	Berlin	FR
157	14/05/1930	AUSTRIA 0-0 ENGLAND	Vienna	FR

THE FIRST WORLD CUP FINALS

The first official World Cup tournament took place in July 1930 in Uruguay, and participation was by invitation only. Economic problems in Europe meant only four teams from that continent travelled to South America. Unofficial champions England, having resigned from FIFA after the arguments over professional football, were not invited to participate, and, in their absence, hosts Uruguay became the first official champions.

158	20/10/1930	ENGLAND 5-1 N. IRELAND	Sheffield	BH
159	22/11/1930	WALES 0-4 ENGLAND	Wrexham	BH
160	28/03/1931	SCOTLAND 2-0 ENGLAND	Glasgow	BH

HALL OF FAME – JOCK THOMSON

Scotland and Celtic goalkeeper **John 'Jock' Thomson** gained four international caps, and won the UFWC with his country in 1931. Born in 1909, Fife-raised Thomson was highly-rated and noted for his bravery. But, just months after the UFWC win, Thomson suffered a tragic injury on the football pitch – fracturing his skull while diving at the feet of an opponent during an Old Firm match on 5 September 1931. He died in Glasgow's Victoria Infirmary later that evening, aged just 22.

161	**16/05/1931**	**AUSTRIA**	**5-0**	**SCOTLAND**	**Vienna**	**FR**
162	24/05/1931	GERMANY	0-6	AUSTRIA	Berlin	FR
163	16/06/1931	AUSTRIA	2-0	SWITZERLAND	Vienna	FR
164	14/09/1931	AUSTRIA	5-0	GERMANY	Vienna	FR
165	04/10/1931	HUNGARY	2-2	AUSTRIA	Budapest	FR
166	29/11/1931	SWITZERLAND	1-8	AUSTRIA	Basel	FR
167	20/03/1932	AUSTRIA	2-1	ITALY	Vienna	FR
168	24/04/1932	AUSTRIA	8-2	HUNGARY	Vienna	FR
169	22/05/1932	CZECH.	1-1	AUSTRIA	Prague	FR
170	17/07/1932	SWEDEN	3-4	AUSTRIA	Stockholm	FR
171	02/10/1932	HUNGARY	2-3	AUSTRIA	Budapest	FR
172	23/10/1932	AUSTRIA	3-1	SWITZERLAND	Vienna	FR
173	**07/12/1932**	**ENGLAND**	**4-3**	**AUSTRIA**	**London**	**FR**
174	01/04/1933	SCOTLAND	2-1	ENGLAND	Glasgow	BH
175	16/09/1933	SCOTLAND	1-2	N IRELAND	Glasgow	BH
176	14/10/1933	N. IRELAND	0-3	ENGLAND	Belfast	BH
177	15/11/1933	ENGLAND	1-2	WALES	Newcastle	BH

THE 1934 WORLD CUP FINALS

Unofficial champions Wales, at odds with FIFA, did not attempt to qualify for the 1934 World Cup finals, and nor did official champs Uruguay. 32 teams entered, 16 qualified, and hosts Italy were the eventual winners.

178	29/09/1934	WALES	0-4	ENGLAND	Cardiff	BH
179	**14/11/1934**	**ENGLAND**	**3-2**	**ITALY**	**London**	**FR**
180	06/02/1935	ENGLAND	2-1	N. IRELAND	Liverpool	BH
181	06/04/1935	SCOTLAND	2-0	ENGLAND	Glasgow	BH
182	05/10/1935	WALES	1-1	SCOTLAND	Cardiff	BH
183	13/11/1935	SCOTLAND	2-1	N. IRELAND	Edinburgh	BH
184	04/04/1936	ENGLAND	1-1	SCOTLAND	London	BH
185	14/10/1936	SCOTLAND	2-0	GERMANY	Glasgow	FR
186	31/10/1936	N. IRELAND	1-3	SCOTLAND	Belfast	BH
187	02/12/1936	SCOTLAND	1-2	WALES	Dundee	BH
188	17/03/1937	WALES	4-1	N IRELAND	Wrexham	BH
189	30/10/1937	WALES	2-1	SCOTLAND	Cardiff	BH
190	17/11/1937	ENGLAND	2-1	WALES	Middlesbrough	BH
191	01/12/1937	ENGLAND	5-4	CZECH.	London	FR
192	09/04/1938	ENGLAND	0-1	SCOTLAND	London	BH
193	**21/05/1938**	**NETHERL.**	**1-3**	**SCOTLAND**	**Amsterdam**	**FR**

THE 1938 WORLD CUP

37 teams entered the third official World Cup tournament, held in France, but unofficial champions Scotland were not involved. Mass withdrawals turned the event into a shambles, as Italy won their second successive World Cup against a backdrop of disorganisation and hullabaloo.

194	08/10/1938	N. IRELAND	0-2	SCOTLAND	Belfast	BH
195	09/11/1938	SCOTLAND	3-2	WALES	Edinburgh	BH
196	07/12/1938	SCOTLAND	3-1	HUNGARY	Glasgow	FR
197	15/04/1939	SCOTLAND	1-2	ENGLAND	Glasgow	BH
198	13/05/1939	ITALY	2-2	ENGLAND	Milan	FR
199	**18/05/1939**	**YUGOSLAVIA**	**2-1**	**ENGLAND**	**Belgrade**	**FR**
200	04/06/1939	YUGOSLAVIA	1-2	ITALY	Belgrade	FR

UNDISPUTED CHAMPIONS

In 1939, World Cup holders and official champions Italy defeated unofficial champions Yugoslavia to become the first side to hold both the World Cup and the UFWC title at the same time. As simultaneous official and unofficial champions, Italy could rightfully claim to be the undisputed football world champions.

201	08/06/1939	HUNGARY	1-3	ITALY	Budapest	FR
202	11/06/1939	ROMANIA	0-1	ITALY	Bucharest	FR
203	20/07/1939	FINLAND	2-3	ITALY	Helsinki	FR

THE SECOND WORLD WAR

World War II kicked off following the Nazi invasion of Poland in September 1939, but international football continued, albeit in reduced circumstances. There would not be another World Cup tournament until 1950, but UFWC lineage continued through the war years, largely involving occupied and neutral countries.

204	12/11/1939	SWITZERLAND	3-1	ITALY	Zurich	FR
205	03/03/1940	ITALY	1-1	SWITZERLAND	Turin	FR
206	31/03/1940	HUNGARY	3-0	SWITZERLAND	Budapest	FR
207	07/04/1940	GERMANY	2-2	HUNGARY	Berlin	FR
208	02/05/1940	HUNGARY	1-0	CROATIA	Budapest	FR
209	19/05/1940	HUNGARY	2-0	ROMANIA	Budapest	FR
210	29/09/1940	HUNGARY	0-0	YUGOSLAVIA	Budapest	FR
211	06/10/1940	HUNGARY	2-2	GERMANY	Budapest	FR
212	01/12/1940	ITALY	1-1	HUNGARY	Genoa	FR
213	08/12/1940	CROATIA	1-1	HUNGARY	Zagreb	FR
214	23/03/1941	YUGOSLAVIA	1-1	HUNGARY	Belgrade	FR
215	06/04/1941	GERMANY	7-0	HUNGARY	Köln	FR
216	20/04/1941	SWITZERLAND	2-1	GERMANY	Berne	FR
217	16/11/1941	SWITZERLAND	1-2	HUNGARY	Zurich	FR
218	03/05/1942	HUNGARY	3-5	GERMANY	Budapest	FR
219	19/07/1942	BULGARIA	0-3	GERMANY	Sofia	FR
220	16/08/1942	GERMANY	7-0	ROMANIA	Beuthen	FR
221	**20/09/1942**	**GERMANY**	**2-3**	**SWEDEN**	**Berlin**	**FR**
222	04/10/1942	SWEDEN	2-1	DENMARK	Solna	FR
223	15/11/1942	SWITZERLAND	3-1	SWEDEN	Zurich	FR

224	04/04/1943	SWITZERLAND	1-0	CROATIA	Zurich	FR
225	16/05/1943	SWITZERLAND	1-3	HUNGARY	Geneva	FR
226	06/06/1943	BULGARIA	2-4	HUNGARY	Sofia	FR
227	12/09/1943	SWEDEN	2-3	HUNGARY	Solna	FR
228	15/09/1943	FINLAND	0-3	HUNGARY	Helsinki	FR
229	07/11/1943	HUNGARY	2-7	SWEDEN	Budapest	FR

FOOTBALL DEFEATED

As the war continued and casualties piled up, international football eventually ground to a halt. There would be no further UFWC matches until after the war in Europe came to an end in May 1945.

230	24/06/1945	SWEDEN	2-1	DENMARK	Solna	FR
231	01/07/1945	DENMARK	3-4	SWEDEN	Copenhagen	FR
232	26/08/1945	SWEDEN	7-2	FINLAND	Gothenburg	FR
233	30/09/1945	FINLAND	1-6	SWEDEN	Helsinki	FR
234	30/09/1945	SWEDEN	4-1	DENMARK	Solna	FR
235	21/10/1945	SWEDEN	10-0	NORWAY	Solna	FR
236	25/11/1945	SWITZERLAND	3-0	SWEDEN	Geneva	FR
237	07/07/1946	SWEDEN	7-2	SWITZERLAND	Stockholm	FR
238	15/09/1946	FINLAND	0-7	SWEDEN	Helsinki	FR
239	15/09/1946	NORWAY	0-3	SWEDEN	Oslo	FR

240	06/10/1946	SWEDEN 3-3 DENMARK	Gothenburg	FR
241	15/06/1947	DENMARK 1-4 SWEDEN	Copenhagen	FR
242	26/06/1947	SWEDEN 6-1 DENMARK	Solna	FR
243	28/06/1947	SWEDEN 5-1 NORWAY	Helsinki	FR
244	24/08/1947	SWEDEN 7-0 FINLAND	Boras	FR
245	14/09/1947	SWEDEN 5-4 POLAND	Solna	FR
246	05/10/1947	SWEDEN 4-1 NORWAY	Stockholm	FR
247	**19/11/1947**	**ENGLAND 4-2 SWEDEN**	**London**	**FR**
248	10/04/1948	SCOTLAND 0-2 ENGLAND	Glasgow	BH
249	16/05/1948	ITALY 0-4 ENGLAND	Turin	FR
250	26/09/1948	DENMARK 0-0 ENGLAND	Copenhagen	FR
251	09/10/1948	N IRELAND 2-6 ENGLAND	Belfast	BH
252	10/11/1948	ENGLAND 1-0 WALES	Birmingham	BH
253	02/12/1948	ENGLAND 6-0 SWITZERLAND	London	FR
254	09/04/1949	ENGLAND 1-3 SCOTLAND	London	BH
255	27/04/1949	SCOTLAND 2-0 FRANCE	Glasgow	FR
256	01/10/1949	N. IRELAND 2-8 SCOTLAND	Belfast	WQ
257	09/11/1949	SCOTLAND 2-0 WALES	Glasgow	WQ
258	15/04/1950	SCOTLAND 0-1 ENGLAND	Glasgow	WQ
259	14/05/1950	PORTUGAL 3-5 ENGLAND	Lisbon	FR

260	18/05/1950	BELGIUM 1-4 ENGLAND	Brussels	FR
261	25/06/1950	ENGLAND 2-0 CHILE	Rio de Janeiro	WC
262	**29/06/1950**	**ENGLAND 0-1 USA**	**Belo Horizonte**	**WC**
263	02/07/1950	USA 2-5 CHILE	Recife	WC

THE 1950 WORLD CUP

For the first time the unofficial champions competed at the official tournament. England were the UFWC champions, but they were relieved of the title by the USA in the first round. The USA – the first UFWC champions from the Americas – lost out to Chile – the first UFWC champs from South America. Uruguay beat Brazil win the tournament and become official champions, but Chile left with the unofficial title.

264	16/03/1952	CHILE 6-1 PANAMA	Santiago	PA
265	26/03/1952	CHILE 4-0 MEXICO	Santiago	PA
266	02/04/1952	CHILE 3-2 PERU	Santiago	PA
267	13/04/1952	CHILE 2-0 URUGUAY	Santiago	PA
268	**20/04/1952**	**CHILE 0-3 BRAZIL**	**Santiago**	**PA**

THE PAN AND SOUTH AMERICAN CHAMPIONSHIPS

The UFWC was contested at the 1952 and 1956 Pan American Championships, and Brazil won both tournaments to become simultaneous UFWC / PA champions. The UFWC was contested at eight South American (Copa America) Championships. Argentina were combined UFWC / CA champions in 1955 and 1993, and Uruguay did the double in 1959.

269	01/03/1953	BRAZIL 8-1 BOLIVIA	Lima	CA
270	12/03/1953	BRAZIL 2-0 ECUADOR	Lima	CA
271	15/03/1953	BRAZIL 1-0 URUGUAY	Lima	CA
272	19/03/1953	PERU 1-0 BRAZIL	Lima	CA
273	**28/03/1953**	**PERU 0-3 URUGUAY**	**Lima**	**CA**
274	31/05/1953	URUGUAY 2-1 ENGLAND	Montevideo	FR
275	10/04/1954	URUGUAY 1-4 PARAGUAY	Montevideo	FR
276	18/04/1954	PARAGUAY 1-1 URUGUAY	Asuncion	FR

THE 1954 WORLD CUP

UFWC title-holders Paraguay failed to qualify for the 1954
World Cup tournament in Switzerland, a tournament won by
West Germany.

277	**02/03/1955**	**PARAGUAY 3-5 ARGENTINA**	**Santiago**	**CA**
278	09/03/1955	ARGENTINA 4-0 ECUADOR	Santiago	CA
279	16/03/1955	ARGENTINA 2-2 PERU	Santiago	CA
280	27/03/1955	ARGENTINA 6-1 URUGUAY	Santiago	CA
281	30/03/1955	CHILE 0-1 ARGENTINA	Santiago	CA
282	22/01/1956	ARGENTINA 2-1 PERU	Montevideo	CA
283	29/01/1956	ARGENTINA 2-0 CHILE	Montevideo	CA
284	01/02/1956	ARGENTINA 1-0 PARAGUAY	Montevideo	CA
285	05/02/1956	ARGENTINA 0-1 BRAZIL	Montevideo	CA

286	10/02/1956	URUGUAY 0-0 BRAZIL	Montevideo	CA
287	01/03/1956	BRAZIL 2-1 CHILE	Mexico City	PA
288	06/03/1956	BRAZIL 1-0 PERU	Mexico City	PA
289	08/03/1956	MEXICO 1-2 BRAZIL	Mexico City	PA
290	13/03/1956	BRAZIL 7-1 COSTA RICA	Mexico City	PA
291	18/03/1956	BRAZIL 2-2 ARGENTINA	Mexico City	PA
292	08/04/1956	PORTUGAL 0-1 BRAZIL	Lisbon	FR
293	11/04/1956	SWITZERLAND 1-1 BRAZIL	Zurich	FR
294	15/04/1956	AUSTRIA 2-3 BRAZIL	Vienna	FR
295	21/04/1956	CZECH 0-0 BRAZIL	Prague	FR
296	25/04/1956	ITALY 3-0 BRAZIL	Milan	FR
297	24/06/1956	ARGENTINA 1-0 ITALY	Buenos Aires	FR
298	01/07/1956	URUGUAY 1-2 ARGENTINA	Montevideo	FR
299	08/07/1956	ARGENTINA 0-0 BRAZIL	Buenos Aires	FR
300	15/08/1956	PARAGUAY 0-1 ARGENTINA	Asuncion	FR
301	19/08/1956	ARGENTINA 1-0 CZECH	Buenos Aires	FR
302	10/10/1956	URUGUAY 1-2 ARGENTINA	Paysandú	FR
303	14/11/1956	ARGENTINA 2-2 URUGUAY	Buenos Aires	FR
304	13/03/1957	ARGENTINA 8-2 COLOMBIA	Lima	CA
305	17/03/1957	ARGENTINA 3-0 ECUADOR	Lima	CA

306	20/03/1957	ARGENTINA 4-0 URUGUAY	Lima	CA
307	28/03/1957	ARGENTINA 6-2 CHILE	Lima	CA
308	03/04/1957	ARGENTINA 3-0 BRAZIL	Lima	CA
309	06/04/1957	PERU 2-1 ARGENTINA	Lima	CA
310	09/04/1957	PERU 1-4 ARGENTINA	Lima	FR
311	23/05/1957	URUGUAY 0-0 ARGENTINA	Montevideo	FR
312	05/06/1957	ARGENTINA 1-1 URUGUAY	Buenos Aires	FR
313	07/07/1957	BRAZIL 1-2 ARGENTINA	Rio de Janeiro	FR
314	10/07/1957	BRAZIL 2-0 ARGENTINA AET	Sao Paulo	FR
315	15/09/1957	CHILE 1-0 BRAZIL	Santiago	FR
316	18/09/1957	CHILE 1-1 BRAZIL AET	Santiago	FR
317	22/09/1957	CHILE 2-1 BOLIVIA	Santiago	WQ
318	29/09/1957	BOLIVIA 3-0 CHILE	La Paz	WQ
319	06/10/1957	BOLIVIA 2-0 ARGENTINA	La Paz	WQ

HALL OF FAME – VICTOR UGARTE

Victor Augustin Ugarte is Bolivia's best-loved footballer and all-time leading goalscorer. He played 45 times for his country between 1947 and 1963, scoring 16 goals. Ugarte captained his side to UFWC glory in 1957 with victories over Chile and Argentina. The impressive 2-0 World Cup qualifier win over mighty Argentina is still celebrated in Bolivia, and Ugarte's brilliant performance saw him christened 'the teacher of Bolivian football'. Born in 1926, Ugarte died in poverty in La Paz in 1995.

320	27/10/1957	ARGENTINA 4-0 BOLIVIA	Buenos Aires	WQ
321	06/04/1958	URUGUAY 1-0 ARGENTINA	Montevideo	FR
322	30/04/1958	ARGENTINA 2-0 URUGUAY	Buenos Aires	FR
323	08/06/1958	ARGENTINA 1-3 W. GERMANY	Malmö	WC
324	11/06/1958	W. GERMANY 2-2 CZECH.	Helsingborg	WC
325	15/06/1958	W. GERMANY 2-2 N. IRELAND	Malmö	WC
326	19/06/1958	W. GERMANY 1-0 YUGOSLAVIA	Malmö	WC
327	24/06/1958	SWEDEN 3-1 W. GERMANY	Gothenburg	WC
328	**29/06/1958**	**SWEDEN 2-5 BRAZIL**	**Solna**	**WC**

THE 1958 WORLD CUP

Not only did UFWC title-holders Germany qualify for the 1958
World Cup finals in Sweden, but the tournament also saw the
first ever combined World Cup final / UFWC title match. The
Germans lost the title to the hosts at the semi-final stage, but
Brazil defeated Sweden in the final to take both the official and
unofficial title and become undisputed champs.

329	10/03/1959	BRAZIL 2-2 PERU	Buenos Aires	CA
330	15/03/1959	BRAZIL 3-0 CHILE	Buenos Aires	CA
331	21/03/1959	BRAZIL 4-2 BOLIVIA	Buenos Aires	CA
332	26/03/1959	BRAZIL 3-1 URUGUAY	Buenos Aires	CA
333	29/03/1959	BRAZIL 4-1 PARAGUAY	Buenos Aires	CA

334	04/04/1959	ARGENTINA	1-1	BRAZIL	Buenos Aires	CA
335	13/05/1959	BRAZIL	2-0	ENGLAND	Rio de Janeiro	FR
336	17/09/1959	BRAZIL	7-0	CHILE	Rio de Janeiro	FR
337	20/09/1959	BRAZIL	1-0	CHILE	Sao Paulo	FR
338	05/12/1959	BRAZIL	3-2	PARAGUAY	Guayaquil	CA

HALL OF FAME – PELÉ

Edson Arantes do Nascimento is popularly regarded as the greatest footballer of all time. Pelè was born in Tres Coracoes, Brazil, in 1940, and has always claimed to dislike his nickname – he punched the schoolchum who invented it and was suspended. In 1958, aged just 17, he became the youngest ever winner of the World Cup, scoring two goals in the World Cup final / UFWC title match for Brazil. He also won the World Cup in 1962 and 1970. He retired from football in 1977 having scored 77 goals in 92 appearances for Brazil, and claiming over 1,000 goals at club level. Although highly regarded as a football ambassador, Pelè was latterly mocked for fronting erectile disfunction ads, and his son Edinho proved to be another source of embarassment. While Pelè sold Viagra, failed goalkeeper Edinho was jailed for trafficking cocaine.

339	12/12/1959	BRAZIL	0-3	URUGUAY	Guayaquil	CA
340	16/12/1959	URUGUAY	5-0	ARGENTINA	Guayaquil	CA
341	22/12/1959	URUGUAY	1-1	PARAGUAY	Guayaquil	CA
342	01/05/1960	CHILE	2-3	URUGUAY	Santiago	FR
343	05/06/1960	URUGUAY	2-2	CHILE	Montevideo	FR

344	09/07/1960	URUGUAY	1-0	BRAZIL	Montevideo	FR
345	13/07/1960	URUGUAY	2-1	PARAGUAY	Montevideo	FR
346	17/08/1960	ARGENTINA	4-0	URUGUAY	Buenos Aires	FR
347	04/12/1960	ECUADOR	3-6	ARGENTINA	Guayaquil	WQ
348	17/12/1960	ARGENTINA	5-0	ECUADOR	Buenos Aires	WQ
349	17/05/1961	PARAGUAY	0-0	ARGENTINA	Asuncion	FR
350	04/06/1961	PORTUGAL	0-2	ARGENTINA	Lisbon	FR
351	11/06/1961	SPAIN	2-0	ARGENTINA	Sevilla	FR

HALL OF FAME – ALFREDO DI STEFANO

Alfredo Di Stefano scored seven goals in seven games for Argentina in 1947 – but 14 years later he scored a goal for Spain that helped deprive Argentina of the UFWC title. Born in Buenos Aires in 1926, Di Stefano began his career at River Plate, before leaving his home country to play club football in Colombia and Spain – most notably for Real Madrid. In 1957 the brilliant striker made his debut for the Spanish national side. And his golden UFWC moment came in 1961, as 35-year-old Di Stefano scored in Spain's 2-0 UFWC win over Argentina. Many Spanish fans still consider Di Stefano to be the greatest footballer of all time.

352	12/11/1961	MOROCCO	0-1	SPAIN	Casablanca	WQ
353	23/11/1961	SPAIN	3-2	MOROCCO	Madrid	WQ
354	10/12/1961	FRANCE	1-1	SPAIN	Colombes	FR
355	31/05/1962	SPAIN	0-1	CZECH.	Viña del Mar	WC

| 356 | 02/06/1962 | CZECH. 0-0 BRAZIL | Viña del Mar | WC |
| 357 | 07/06/1962 | CZECH. 1-3 MEXICO | Viña del Mar | WC |

THE 1962 WORLD CUP

UFWC champions Spain qualified for the 1962 finals, but lost the title to Czechoslovakia, who in turn lost it to Mexico, who were dumped out of the competition at the group stage. Brazil won the tournament, in Chile.

358	**24/03/1963**	**MEXICO 1-2 D ANTILLES**	**Santa Ana**	**CC**
359	28/03/1963	D. ANTILLES 0-1 COSTA RICA	Santa Ana	CC
360	30/03/1963	COSTA RICA 0-0 MEXICO	Santa Ana	CC
361	03/04/1963	EL SALVADOR 1-4 COSTA RICA	S. Salvador	CC
362	05/04/1963	COSTA RICA 1-0 D. ANTILLES	S. Salvador	CC
363	07/04/1963	COSTA RICA 2-1 HONDURAS	S. Salvador	CC

THE CONCACAF CHAMPIONSHIP

The Confederation of North, Central American and Caribbean Association Football (CONCACAF) was formed in 1961, and the first CONCACAF Championships took place in 1963. Unofficial champions Costa Rica, 'Los Ticos', won the tournament that year to secure a UFWC / CC double. It was the only occasion the UFWC title was contested at the CONCACAF tournament, now known as the CONCACAF Gold Cup.

| 364 | 01/09/1963 | COLOMBIA 4-5 COSTA RICA | Bogota | FR |
| 365 | 04/09/1963 | COLOMBIA 1-0 COSTA RICA | Cali | FR |

366	20/06/1965	COLOMBIA	0-1	ECUADOR	Barranquilla	WQ
367	25/06/1965	ECUADOR	2-0	COLOMBIA	Guayaquil	WQ
368	15/08/1965	ECUADOR	2-2	CHILE	Guayaquil	WQ
369	22/08/1965	CHILE	3-1	ECUADOR	Santiago	WQ
370	12/10/1965	CHILE	2-1	ECUADOR	Lima	WQ
371	23/02/1966	CHILE	0-2	USSR	Santiago	FR
372	20/04/1966	SWITZERLAND	2-2	USSR	Basel	FR
373	24/04/1966	AUSTRIA	0-1	USSR	Vienna	FR
374	18/05/1966	CZECH.	1-2	USSR	Prague	FR
375	22/05/1966	BELGIUM	0-1	USSR	Brussels	FR
376	05/06/1966	USSR	3-3	FRANCE	Moscow	FR
377	12/07/1966	USSR	3-0	KOREA	Middlesbrough	WC
378	16/07/1966	USSR	1-0	ITALY	Sunderland	WC
379	20/07/1966	USSR	2-1	CHILE	Sunderland	WC
380	23/07/1966	USSR	2-1	HUNGARY	Sunderland	WC
381	25/07/1966	USSR	1-2	W. GERMANY	Liverpool	WC
382	**30/07/1966**	**ENGLAND**	**4-2**	**W. GERMANY AET**	**London**	**WC**

THE 1966 WORLD CUP

The USSR took the unofficial title into the official 1966 competition, but lost it to West Germany in the semi-final. Hosts England defeated West Germany in the final to win both the official and official titles.

HALL OF FAME – GEOFF HURST

Sir Geoffrey Charles Hurst scored a famous hat-trick in the combined 1966 World Cup / UFWC title match. No other player has ever scored a hat-trick at such a level. He scored 24 goals in 49 games for England over his international career, and hit 252 goals in 499 games at club level for West Ham United. He was knighted in 1998, and later took up the odd-sounding position of Director of Football for burger kings McDonald's.

383	**22/10/1966**	**N. IRELAND**	**0-2**	**ENGLAND**	**Belfast**	**EQ**
384	02/11/1966	ENGLAND	0-0	CZECH.	London	FR
385	16/11/1966	ENGLAND	5-1	WALES	London	EQ
386	**15/04/1967**	**ENGLAND**	**2-3**	**SCOTLAND**	**London**	**EQ**
387	10/05/1967	SCOTLAND	0-2	USSR	Glasgow	FR
388	28/05/1967	USSR	2-0	MEXICO	Leningrad	FR
389	03/06/1967	FRANCE	2-4	USSR	Paris	FR
390	11/06/1967	USSR	4-3	AUSTRIA	Moscow	EQ
391	16/07/1967	USSR	4-0	GREECE	Moscow	EQ
392	30/08/1967	USSR	2-0	FINLAND	Moscow	EQ
393	06/09/1967	FINLAND	2-5	USSR	Turku	EQ
394	01/10/1967	USSR	2-2	SWITZERLAND	Moscow	FR
395	08/10/1967	BULGARIA	1-2	USSR	Sofia	FR
396	15/10/1967	AUSTRIA	1-0	USSR	Vienna	EQ

397	05/11/1967	**AUSTRIA 1-1 GREECE ABA**	**Vienna**	**EQ**
398	01/05/1968	AUSTRIA 1-1 ROMANIA	Linz	FR
399	19/05/1968	AUSTRIA 7-1 CYPRUS	Vienna	EQ
400	16/06/1968	USSR 3-1 AUSTRIA	Leningrad	FR
401	01/08/1968	SWEDEN 2-2 USSR	Gothenburg	FR
402	20/02/1969	COLOMBIA 1-3 USSR	Bogota	FR
403	25/07/1969	E. GERMANY 2-2 USSR	Leipzig	FR
404	06/08/1969	USSR 0-1 SWEDEN	Moscow	FR
405	25/08/1969	SWEDEN 3-1 ISRAEL	Solna	FR
406	24/09/1969	SWEDEN 2-0 HUNGARY	Solna	FR
407	15/10/1969	SWEDEN 2-0 FRANCE	Solna	WQ
408	01/11/1969	FRANCE 3-0 SWEDEN	Paris	WQ
409	08/04/1970	FRANCE 1-1 BULGARIA	Rouen	FR
410	28/04/1970	FRANCE 2-0 ROMANIA	Reims	FR
411	03/05/1970	SWITZERLAND 2-1 FRANCE	Basel	FR

THE 1970 WORLD CUP

UFWC champs Switzerland failed to qualify for the 1970 World Cup tournament, held in Mexico and won by Brazil.

412	17/10/1970	SWITZERLAND 1-1 ITALY	Berne	FR

413	15/11/1970	SWITZERLAND	0-1	HUNGARY	Basel	FR
414	04/04/1971	AUSTRIA	0-2	HUNGARY	Vienna	FR
415	24/04/1971	HUNGARY	1-1	FRANCE	Budapest	EQ
416	19/05/1971	BULGARIA	3-0	HUNGARY	Sofia	EQ
417	09/06/1971	NORWAY	1-4	BULGARIA	Oslo	EQ
418	25/09/1971	HUNGARY	2-0	BULGARIA	Budapest	EQ
419	09/10/1971	FRANCE	0-2	HUNGARY	Colombes	EQ
420	27/10/1971	HUNGARY	4-0	NORWAY	Budapest	EQ
421	14/11/1971	MALTA	0-2	HUNGARY	Valetta	WQ
422	12/01/1972	SPAIN	1-0	HUNGARY	Madrid	FR
423	16/02/1972	N. IRELAND	1-1	SPAIN	Hull	EQ
424	12/04/1972	GREECE	0-0	SPAIN	Salonika	FR
425	23/05/1972	SPAIN	2-0	URUGUAY	Madrid	FR
426	11/10/1972	SPAIN	1-0	ARGENTINA	Madrid	FR
427	19/10/1972	SPAIN	2-2	YUGOSLAVIA	G. Canaria	WQ
428	17/01/1973	GREECE	2-3	SPAIN	Athens	WQ
429	21/02/1973	SPAIN	3-1	GREECE	Malaga	WQ
430	02/05/1973	NETHERL.	3-2	SPAIN	Amsterdam	FR
431	22/08/1973	NETHERL.	5-0	ICELAND	Amsterdam	WQ
432	29/08/1973	ICELAND	1-8	NETHERL.	Deventer	WQ

433	12/09/1973	NORWAY	1-2	NETHERLANDS	Oslo	WQ
434	10/10/1973	NETHERL.	1-1	POLAND	Rotterdam	FR
435	18/11/1973	NETHERL.	0-0	BELGIUM	Amsterdam	WQ
436	27/03/1974	NETHERL.	1-1	AUSTRIA	Rotterdam	FR
437	26/05/1974	NETHERL.	4-1	ARGENTINA	Amsterdam	FR
438	05/06/1974	NETHERL.	0-0	ROMANIA	Rotterdam	FR
439	15/06/1974	NETHERL.	2-0	URUGUAY	Hannover	WC
440	19/06/1974	NETHERL.	0-0	SWEDEN	Dortmund	WC
441	23/06/1974	NETHERL.	4-1	BULGARIA	Dortmund	WC
442	26/06/1974	NETHERL.	4-0	ARGENTINA	G.kirchen	WC
443	30/06/1974	NETHERL.	2-0	E. GERMANY	G.kirchen	WC
444	**03/07/1974**	**NETHERL.**	**2-0**	**BRAZIL**	**Dortmund**	**WC**
445	**07/07/1974**	**W. GERMANY**	**2-1**	**NETHERL.**	**Munich**	**WC**

HALL OF FAME – FRANZ BECKENBAUER

Franz Beckenbauer, 'Der Kaiser', was probably the best 'libero' football has ever seen. Born in 1945, Beckenbauer is the only man to have won the World Cup both as a player and as a manager. He remains a legend in Germany, despite some un-welcome tabloid adventures. 'He's got away with everything that a German man shouldn't be allowed to get away with,' said former teammate Paul Breitner. 'He got divorced, left his chil-dren, took off with his girlfriend, got into trouble with tax col-lectors, left his girlfriend again. But he's forgiven for everything because he's got a good heart, he's a positive person and he's always ready to help.'

THE 1974 WORLD CUP

The Netherlands were longstanding unofficial champions going into the 1974 official tournament, and they made it all the way to the final, before being stopped by hosts West Germany. The Germans took both the official and unofficial titles with a 2-1 win.

446	04/09/1974	SWITZERLAND	1-2	W. GERMANY	Basel	FR
447	20/11/1974	GREECE	2-2	W. GERMANY	Piraeus	EQ
448	22/12/1974	MALTA	0-1	W. GERMANY	Gzira	EQ
449	12/03/1975	ENGLAND	2-0	W. GERMANY	London	FR
450	16/04/1975	ENGLAND	5-0	CYPRUS	London	EQ
451	11/05/1975	CYPRUS	0-1	ENGLAND	Limassol	EQ
452	17/05/1975	N. IRELAND	0-0	ENGLAND	Belfast	BH
453	21/05/1975	ENGLAND	2-2	WALES	London	BH
454	24/05/1975	ENGLAND	5-1	SCOTLAND	London	BH
455	03/09/1975	SWITZERLAND	1-2	ENGLAND	Basel	FR
456	30/10/1975	CZECH.	2-1	ENGLAND	Bratislava	EQ
457	12/11/1975	PORTUGAL	1-1	CZECH.	Porto	EQ
458	23/11/1975	CYPRUS	0-3	CZECH.	Limassol	EQ
459	10/03/1976	CZECH.	2-2	USSR	Kosice	FR
460	27/03/1976	FRANCE	2-2	CZECH.	Paris	FR
461	24/04/1976	CZECH.	2-0	USSR	Bratislava	EQ

462	22/05/1976	USSR 2-2 CZECH.	Kiev	EQ
463	16/06/1976	CZECH. 3-1 NETHERLANDS AET	Zagreb	EC
464	**20/06/1976**	**CZECH.* 2-2 W. GERMANY PEN**	**Belgrade**	**EC**

THE EUROPEAN CHAMPIONSHIPS

The Union of European Football Associations (UEFA) formed in 1954, and organised the first European Championships in 1960. Although the UFWC title had previously been contested during qualifying, it was first contested at the actual Euro tournament in 1976, when unofficial champs Czechoslovakia beat West Germany to become joint UFWC / EC champions. The UFWC title was again contested alongside the European Championships in 1982, with France winning both honours, in 1996, when Germany won the combined final, and 2000, with France again doing the double.

465	22/09/1976	ROMANIA 1-1 CZECH.	Bucharest	FR
466	06/10/1976	CZECH. 3-2 ROMANIA	Prague	FR
467	13/10/1976	CZECH. 2-0 SCOTLAND	Prague	WQ
468	17/11/1976	W. GERMANY 2-0 CZECH.	Hannover	FR
469	23/02/1977	FRANCE 1-0 W. GERMANY	Paris	FR
470	30/03/1977	REP. IRELAND 1-0 FRANCE	Dublin	WQ
471	24/04/1977	REP. IRELAND 0-0 POLAND	Dublin	FR
472	01/06/1977	BULGARIA 2-1 REP. IRELAND	Sofia	WQ
473	21/09/1977	BULGARIA 3-1 TURKEY	Sofia	FR

474	12/10/1977	REP. IRELAND 0-0 BULGARIA	Dublin	WQ
475	26/10/1977	BULGARIA 0-0 GREECE	Sofia	FR
476	16/11/1977	FRANCE 3-1 BULGARIA	Paris	WQ
477	08/02/1978	ITALY 2-2 FRANCE	Naples	FR
478	08/03/1978	FRANCE 2-0 PORTUGAL	Paris	FR
479	01/04/1978	FRANCE 1-0 BRAZIL	Paris	FR
480	11/05/1978	FRANCE 2-1 IRAN	Toulouse	FR
481	19/05/1978	FRANCE 2-0 TUNISIA	Ville. d'Ascq	FR
482	02/06/1978	FRANCE 1-2 ITALY	Mar del Plata	WC
483	06/06/1978	ITALY 3-1 HUNGARY	Mar del Plata	WC
484	10/06/1978	ARGENTINA 0-1 ITALY	Buenos Aires	WC
485	14/06/1978	ITALY 0-0 W. GERMANY	B. Aires	WC
486	18/06/1978	ITALY 1-0 AUSTRIA	B. Aires	WC
487	21/06/1978	ITALY 1-2 NETHERL.	B. Aires	WC
488	**25/06/1978**	**ARGENTINA 3-1 NETHERL.**	**AET B. Aires**	**WC**

THE 1978 WORLD CUP

The UFWC title changed hands three times during the 1978 FIFA tournament. First, unofficial champs France lost out to Italy. Next, Italy gave up the title to the Netherlands. Then, in the World Cup final, the Netherlands were beaten by hosts Argentina. Official and unofficial football champions Argentina were indisputably the best side in the world.

489	25/04/1979	ARGENTINA	2-1	BULGARIA		B. Aires	FR
490	22/05/1979	ARGENTINA*	0-0	NETHERL.	PEN	Berne	FR
491	26/05/1979	ITALY	2-2	ARGENTINA		Rome	FR
492	02/06/1979	SCOTLAND	1-3	ARGENTINA		Glasgow	FR
493	18/07/1979	BOLIVIA	2-1	ARGENTINA		La Paz	CA
494	26/07/1979	BOLIVIA	2-1	BRAZIL		La Paz	CA
495	01/08/1979	PARAGUAY	2-0	BOLIVIA		Asuncion	FR
496	29/08/1979	ECUADOR	1-2	PARAGUAY		Quito	CA
497	13/09/1979	PARAGUAY	2-0	ECUADOR		Asuncion	CA
498	20/09/1979	PARAGUAY	0-0	URUGUAY		Asuncion	CA
499	26/09/1979	URUGUAY	2-2	PARAGUAY		Montevideo	CA
500	10/10/1979	PERU	2-3	PARAGUAY		Lima	FR
501	24/10/1979	PARAGUAY	2-1	BRAZIL		Asuncion	CA
502	31/10/1979	BRAZIL	2-2	PARAGUAY		Rio de Jan.	CA
503	28/11/1979	PARAGUAY	3-0	CHILE		Asuncion	CA
504	05/12/1979	CHILE	1-0	PARAGUAY		Santiago	CA
505	11/12/1979	CHILE	0-0	PARAGUAY		B. Aires	CA
506	24/06/1980	BRAZIL	2-1	CHILE		Belo Horiz.	FR
507	29/06/1980	BRAZIL	1-1	POLAND		Sao Paulo	FR
508	27/08/1980	BRAZIL	1-0	URUGUAY		Fortaleza	FR

509	25/09/1980	PARAGUAY 1-2 BRAZIL	Asuncion	FR
510	30/10/1980	BRAZIL 6-0 PARAGUAY	Goiânia	FR
511	21/12/1980	BRAZIL 2-0 SWITZERLAND	Cuiabá	FR
512	04/01/1981	BRAZIL 1-1 ARGENTINA	Montevideo	FR
513	07/01/1981	BRAZIL 4-1 W. GERMANY	Montevideo	FR
514	10/01/1981	URUGUAY 2-1 BRAZIL	Montevideo	FR
515	29/04/1981	CHILE 1-2 URUGUAY	Santiago	FR
516	15/07/1981	URUGUAY 0-0 CHILE	Montevideo	FR
517	09/08/1981	URUGUAY 3-2 COLOMBIA	Montevideo	WQ
518	23/08/1981	URUGUAY 1-2 PERU	Montevideo	WQ
519	06/09/1981	PERU 0-0 URUGUAY	Lima	WQ
520	23/03/1982	CHILE 2-1 PERU	Santiago	FR
521	30/03/1982	PERU 1-0 CHILE	Lima	FR
522	18/04/1982	HUNGARY 1-2 PERU	Budapest	FR
523	25/04/1982	ALGERIA 1-1 PERU	Algiers	FR
524	28/04/1982	FRANCE 0-1 PERU	Paris	FR
525	17/05/1982	PERU 2-0 ROMANIA	Lima	FR
526	15/06/1982	PERU 0-0 CAMEROON	La Coruna	WC
527	18/06/1982	PERU 1-1 ITALY	Vigo	WC
528	22/06/1982	PERU 1-5 POLAND	La Coruna	WC

529	28/06/1982	POLAND 3-0 BELGIUM	Barcelona	WC
530	04/07/1982	POLAND 0-0 USSR	Barcelona	WC
531	08/07/1982	POLAND 0-2 ITALY	Barcelona	WC
532	**11/07/1982**	**ITALY 3-1 W. GERMANY**	**Madrid**	**WC**

THE 1982 WORLD CUP

For the third time running, the UFWC title was contested at the World Cup finals. Peru travelled to Spain as unofficial champions, but they lost the title to Poland, who in turn lost out to Italy. Unofficial champions Italy held off West Germany in the final match to take the official title and become undisputed champions – the second time the Italians held both titles simultaneously.

533	27/10/1982	ITALY 0-1 SWITZERLAND	Rome	FR
534	17/11/1982	SWITZERLAND 2-0 SCOTLAND	Berne	EQ
535	01/12/1982	GREECE 1-3 SWITZERLAND	Athens	FR
536	07/03/1983	BULGARIA 1-1 SWITZERLAND	Varna	FR
537	30/03/1983	SCOTLAND 2-2 SWITZERLAND	Glasgow	EQ
538	13/04/1983	SWITZERLAND 0-1 USSR	Lausanne	FR
539	27/04/1983	USSR 5-0 PORTUGAL	Moscow	EQ
540	17/05/1983	AUSTRIA 2-2 USSR	Vienna	FR
541	22/05/1983	POLAND 1-1 USSR	Chorzow	EQ
542	01/06/1983	FINLAND 0-1 USSR	Helsinki	EQ

543	26/07/1983	E. GERMANY 1-3 USSR	Leipzig	FR
544	09/10/1983	USSR 2-0 POLAND	Moscow	EQ
545	13/11/1983	PORTUGAL 1-0 USSR	Lisbon	EQ
546	02/06/1984	PORTUGAL 2-3 YUGOSLAVIA	Lisbon	FR
547	07/06/1984	SPAIN 0-1 YUGOSLAVIA	La Linea	FR
548	13/06/1984	YUGOSLAVIA 0-2 BELGIUM	Lens	EC
549	16/06/1984	FRANCE 5-0 BELGIUM	Nantes	EC
550	19/06/1984	FRANCE 3-2 YUGOSLAVIA	St Etienne	EC
551	23/06/1984	FRANCE 3-2 PORTUGAL AET	Marseilles	EC
552	**27/06/1984**	**FRANCE 2-0 SPAIN**	**Paris**	**EC**
553	13/10/1984	LUXEMBOURG 0-4 FRANCE	Luxembourg	WQ
554	21/11/1984	FRANCE 1-0 BULGARIA	Paris	WQ
555	08/12/1984	FRANCE 2-0 E. GERMANY	Paris	WQ
556	03/04/1985	YUGOSLAVIA 0-0 FRANCE	Sarajevo	WQ
557	02/05/1985	BULGARIA 2-0 FRANCE	Sofia	WQ
558	03/06/1985	BULGARIA 2-1 YUGOSLAVIA	Sofia	WQ
559	27/08/1985	MEXICO 1-1 BULGARIA	Los Angeles	FR
560	04/09/1985	NETHERL. 1-0 BULGARIA	Heerenveen	FR
561	16/10/1985	BELGIUM 1-0 NETHERL.	Brussels	WQ
562	20/11/1985	NETHERL. 2-1 BELGIUM	Rotterdam	WQ

563	12/03/1986	E. GERMANY	0-1	NETHERLANDS	Leipzig	FR
564	29/04/1986	NETHERL.	0-0	SCOTLAND	Eindhoven	FR
565	14/05/1986	W. GERMANY	3-1	NETHERLANDS	Dortmund	FR
566	04/06/1986	W. GERMANY	1-1	URUGUAY	Queretaro	WC
567	08/06/1986	W. GERMANY	2-1	SCOTLAND	Queretaro	WC
568	13/06/1986	W. GERMANY	0-2	DENMARK	Queretaro	WC
569	18/06/1986	DENMARK	1-5	SPAIN	Queretaro	WC
570	22/06/1986	SPAIN	1-1	BELGIUM* PEN	Puebla	WC
571	25/06/1986	BELGIUM	0-2	ARGENTINA	Mex. City	WC
572	29/06/1986	ARGENTINA	3-2	W GERMANY	Mex. City	WC

THE 1986 WORLD CUP

West Germany held the UFWC title at the beginning of Mexico 86, but Argentina eventually came out on top to become undisputed official and unofficial champions.

HALL OF FAME - DIEGO MARADONA

Diego Armando Maradona was born in Buenos Aires in 1960. He played for Argentina at four World Cup finals, winning the 1986 tournament, and became regarded as perhaps the greatest footballer ever. However he also became regarded as football's most notorious cheat following the infamous 'Hand of God' incident, and various doping scandals. Post-retirement he fought drug addiction and defied severe health problems to become Argentina's most popular TV presenter.

573	10/06/1987	ARGENTINA 1-3 ITALY	Zurich	FR
574	23/09/1987	ITALY 1-0 YUGOSLAVIA	Pisa	FR
575	17/10/1987	SWITZERLAND 0-0 ITALY	Berne	EQ
576	14/11/1987	ITALY 2-1 SWEDEN	Naples	EQ
577	05/12/1987	ITALY 3-0 PORTUGAL	Milan	EQ
578	20/02/1988	ITALY 4-1 USSR	Bari	FR
579	31/03/1988	YUGOSLAVIA 1-1 ITALY	Split	FR
580	27/04/1988	LUXEMBOURG 0-3 ITALY	Luxembourg	FR
581	**04/06/1988**	**ITALY 0-1 WALES**	**Brescia**	**FR**
582	14/09/1988	NETHERL. 1-0 WALES	Amsterdam	WQ
583	19/10/1988	W. GERMANY 0-0 NETHERL.	Munich	WQ
584	16/11/1988	ITALY 1-0 NETHERL.	Rome	FR
585	22/12/1988	ITALY 2-0 SCOTLAND	Perugia	FR
586	22/02/1989	ITALY 1-0 DENMARK	Pisa	FR
587	25/03/1989	AUSTRIA 0-1 ITALY	Vienna	FR
588	29/03/1989	ROMANIA 1-0 ITALY	Sibiu	FR
589	12/04/1989	POLAND 2-1 ROMANIA	Warsaw	FR
590	02/05/1989	NORWAY 0-3 POLAND	Oslo	FR
591	07/05/1989	SWEDEN 2-1 POLAND	Solna	WQ
592	31/05/1989	SWEDEN 2-0 ALGERIA	Orebro	FR

593	14/06/1989	DENMARK	6-0	SWEDEN	Copenhagen	FR
594	18/06/1989	DENMARK	4-0	BRAZIL	Copenhagen	FR
595	23/08/1989	BELGIUM	3-0	DENMARK	Bruges	FR
596	06/09/1989	BELGIUM	3-0	PORTUGAL	Brussels	WQ
597	11/10/1989	SWITZERLAND	2-2	BELGIUM	Basel	WQ
598	25/10/1989	BELGIUM	1-1	LUXEMBOURG	Brussels	WQ
599	17/01/1990	GREECE	2-0	BELGIUM	Athens	FR
600	28/03/1990	GREECE	2-1	ISRAEL	Athens	FR
601	30/05/1990	ITALY	0-0	GREECE	Perugia	FR

THE 1990 WORLD CUP

UFWC champions Greece failed to qualify for Italia 90, finishing below Romania and Denmark in their qualifying group, meaning that the unofficial title was not contested at the official tournament.

602	05/09/1990	GREECE	1-0	ALBANIA	Patra	FR
603	10/10/1990	GREECE	6-1	EGYPT	Athens	FR
604	31/10/1990	GREECE	4-0	MALTA	Athens	EQ
605	21/11/1990	NETHERL.	2-0	GREECE	Rotterdam	EQ
606	19/12/1990	MALTA	0-8	NETHERL.	Valetta	EQ
607	13/03/1991	NETHERL.	1-0	MALTA	Rotterdam	EQ
608	17/04/1991	NETHERL.	2-0	FINLAND	Rotterdam	EQ

609	05/06/1991	FINLAND	1-1	NETHERL.		Helsinki	EQ
610	11/09/1991	NETHERL.	1-1	POLAND		Eindhoven	FR
611	16/10/1991	NETHERL.	1-0	PORTUGAL		Rotterdam	EQ
612	04/02/1992	GREECE	0-2	NETHERL.		Salonika	EQ
613	13/02/1992	PORTUGAL	2-0	NETHERL.		Faro	FR
614	31/05/1992	PORTUGAL	0-0	ITALY		New Haven	FR
615	04/06/1992	USA	1-0	PORTUGAL		Chicago	FR
616	06/06/1992	USA	1-1	ITALY		Chicago	FR
617	14/06/1992	USA	0-1	AUSTRALIA		Orlando	FR
618	18/06/1992	ARGENTINA	2-0	AUSTRALIA		B. Aires	FR
619	23/09/1992	URUGUAY	0-0	ARGENTINA		Montevideo	FR
620	16/10/1992	ARGENTINA	4-0	IVORY COAST		Riyadh	FR
621	20/10/1992	SAUDI ARABIA	1-3	ARGENTINA		Riyadh	FR
622	26/11/1992	ARGENTINA	2-0	POLAND		B. Aires	FR
623	18/02/1993	ARGENTINA	1-1	BRAZIL		B. Aires	FR
624	24/02/1993	ARGENTINA*	1-1	DENMARK	PEN	Mar Del P.	FR
625	17/06/1993	ARGENTINA	1-0	BOLIVIA		Guayaquil	CA
626	20/06/1993	ARGENTINA	1-1	MEXICO		Guayaquil	CA
627	23/06/1993	ARGENTINA	1-1	COLOMBIA		Guayaquil	CA
628	27/06/1993	ARGENTINA*	1-1	BRAZIL	PEN	Guayaquil	CA

629	01/07/1993	ARGENTINA* 0-0 COLOMBIA	PEN	Guayaquil	CA
630	**04/07/1993**	**ARGENTINA 2-1 MEXICO**		**Guayaquil**	**CA**
631	01/08/1993	PERU 0-1 ARGENTINA		Lima	WQ
632	08/08/1993	PARAGUAY 1-3 ARGENTINA		Asuncion	WQ
633	15/08/1993	COLOMBIA 2-1 ARGENTINA		Barranquilla	WQ
634	22/08/1993	PARAGUAY 1-1 COLOMBIA		Asuncion	WQ
635	29/08/1993	COLOMBIA 4-0 PERU		Barranquilla	WQ
636	05/09/1993	ARGENTINA 0-5 COLOMBIA		B. Aires	WQ
637	28/01/1994	VENEZUELA 1-2 COLOMBIA		Barinas	FR
638	06/02/1994	SAUDI ARABIA 1-1 COLOMBIA		Jeddah	FR
639	10/02/1994	SAUDI ARABIA 0-1 COLOMBIA		Jeddah	FR
640	18/02/1994	COLOMBIA 0-0 SWEDEN		Miami	FR
641	20/02/1994	COLOMBIA 2-0 BOLIVIA		Miami	FR
642	26/02/1994	COLOMBIA 2-2 DPR KOREA		Monterrey	FR
643	02/03/1994	MEXICO 0-0 COLOMBIA		Mexico City	FR
644	07/04/1994	COLOMBIA 0-1 BOLIVIA		Villavicenico	FR
645	20/04/1994	ROMANIA 3-0 BOLIVIA		Bucharest	FR
646	24/05/1994	ROMANIA 2-0 NIGERIA		Bucharest	FR
647	01/06/1994	ROMANIA 0-0 SLOVENIA		Bucharest	FR
648	12/06/1994	ROMANIA 1-1 SWEDEN		Mision Viejo	FR

649	18/06/1994	ROMANIA 3-1 COLOMBIA	L.A.	WC
650	22/06/1994	ROMANIA 1-4 SWITZERLAND	Detroit	WC
651	**26/06/1994**	**SWITZERLAND 0-2 COLOMBIA**	**San Fran.**	**WC**

THE 1994 WORLD CUP

Romania lost the UFWC title to Switzerland at USA 94, but Switzerland immediately lost it to Colombia in their final group match. But that was Colombia's only win at the tournament and, finishing bottom of group A, the Colombians went home, taking the UFWC title with them. And the UFWC title was temporarily put into mothballs. The murder of Andres Escobar meant that Colombia would not play another game for a full seven months.

652	31/01/1995	COLOMBIA 0-1 S. KOREA	Hong Kong	FR
653	04/02/1995	SOUTH KOREA 0-1 YUGOSLAVIA	Hong Kong	FR
654	31/03/1995	YUGOSLAVIA 1-0 URUGUAY	Belgrade	FR
655	31/05/1995	YUGOSLAVIA 1-2 RUSSIA	Belgrade	FR
656	07/06/1995	SAN MARINO 0-7 RUSSIA	Serravalle	EQ
657	16/08/1995	FINLAND 0-6 RUSSIA	Helsinki	EQ
658	06/09/1995	FAROE ISLES 2-5 RUSSIA	Toftir	EQ
659	11/10/1995	RUSSIA 2-1 GREECE	Moscow	EQ
660	15/11/1995	RUSSIA 3-1 FINLAND	Moscow	EQ
661	07/02/1996	MALTA 0-2 RUSSIA	Ta'quali	FR

662	09/02/1996	RUSSIA 3-0 ICELAND	Ta'quali	FR
663	11/02/1996	RUSSIA 3-1 SLOVENIA	Ta'quali	FR
664	27/03/1996	REP. IRELAND 0-2 RUSSIA	Dublin	FR
665	24/04/1996	BELGIUM 0-0 RUSSIA	Brussels	FR
666	25/05/1996	QUATAR 2-5 RUSSIA	Doha	FR
667	29/05/1996	RUSSIA 1-0 UAE	Moscow	FR
668	02/06/1996	RUSSIA 2-0 POLAND	Moscow	FR
669	11/06/1996	ITALY 2-1 RUSSIA	Liverpool	EC
670	14/06/1996	CZECH REP. 2-1 ITALY	Liverpool	EC
671	19/06/1996	RUSSIA 3-3 CZECH REP.	Liverpool	EC
672	23/06/1996	PORTUGAL 0-1 CZECH REP.	Birmingham	EC
673	26/06/1996	FRANCE 0-0 CZECH REP.* PEN	Manchester	EC
674	**30/06/1996**	**CZECH REP. 1-2 GERMANY AET London**		**EC**
675	04/09/1996	POLAND 0-2 GERMANY	Zabrze	FR
676	09/10/1996	ARMENIA 1-5 GERMANY	Yerevan	WQ
677	09/11/1996	GERMANY 1-1 N IRELAND	Nuremburg	WQ
678	14/12/1996	PORTUGAL 0-0 GERMANY	Lisbon	WQ
679	26/02/1997	ISRAEL 0-1 GERMANY	Tel Aviv	FR
680	02/04/1997	ALBANIA 2-3 GERMANY	Granada	WQ
681	30/04/1997	GERMANY 2-0 UKRAINE	Bremen	WQ

682	07/06/1997	UKRAINE	0-0 GERMANY	Kiev		WQ
683	20/08/1997	N. IRELAND	1-3 GERMANY	Belfast		WQ
684	06/09/1997	GERMANY	1-1 PORTUGAL	Berlin		WQ
685	10/09/1997	GERMANY	4-0 ARMENIA	Dortmund		WQ
686	11/10/1997	GERMANY	4-3 ALBANIA	Hannover		WQ
687	15/11/1997	GERMANY	3-0 S. AFRICA	Dusseldorf		FR
688	18/02/1998	OMAN	0-2 GERMANY	Muscat		FR
689	22/02/1998	SAUDI ARABIA	0-3 GERMANY	Riyadh		FR
690	25/03/1998	GERMANY	1-2 BRAZIL	Suttgart		FR
691	29/04/1998	BRAZIL	0-1 ARGENTINA	Rio de Jan.		FR
692	14/05/1998	ARGENTINA	5-0 BOSNIA-HERZ.	Cordoba		FR
693	19/05/1998	ARGENTINA	1-0 CHILE	Mendoza		FR
694	25/05/1998	ARGENTINA	2-0 S. AFRICA	B. Aires		FR
695	14/06/1998	ARGENTINA	1-0 JAPAN	Toulouse		WC
696	21/06/1998	ARGENTINA	5-0 JAMAICA	Paris		WC
697	26/06/1998	ARGENTINA	1-0 CROATIA	Bordeaux		WC
698	30/06/1998	ARGENTINA*	2-2 ENGLAND	PEN	St Etienne	WC
699	04/07/1998	ARGENTINA	1-2 NETHERL.		Marseilles	WC
700	07/07/1998	NETHERL.	1-1 BRAZIL*	PEN	Marseilles	WC
701	**12/07/1998**	**FRANCE**	**3-0 BRAZIL**		**St Denis**	**WC**

THE 1998 WORLD CUP

Argentina took the unofficial title to France 98, and held on to it all the way to the quarter finals. Then the Netherlands intervened. But Brazil beat the Dutch in the semi-final. Then, in a combined World Cup final / UFWC title match, France comprehensively defeated Brazil to win both the official and unofficial titles.

702	19/08/1998	AUSTRIA 2-2 FRANCE	Vienna	FR
703	05/09/1998	ICELAND 1-1 FRANCE	Reykjavik	EQ
704	10/10/1998	RUSSIA 2-3 FRANCE	Moscow	EQ
705	14/10/1998	FRANCE 2-0 ANDORRA	St Denis	EQ
706	20/01/1999	FRANCE 1-0 MOROCCO	Marseilles	FR
707	10/02/1999	ENGLAND 0-2 FRANCE	London	FR
708	27/03/1999	FRANCE 0-0 UKRAINE	St Denis	EQ
709	31/03/1999	FRANCE 2-0 ARMENIA	St Denis	EQ
710	05/06/1999	FRANCE 2-3 RUSSIA	St Denis	EQ
711	09/06/1999	RUSSIA 1-0 ICELAND	Moscow	EQ
712	18/08/1999	BELARUS 0-2 RUSSIA	Minsk	FR
713	04/09/1999	RUSSIA 2-0 ARMENIA	Moscow	EQ
714	08/09/1999	ANDORRA 1-2 RUSSIA	Andorra la Vella	EQ
715	09/10/1999	RUSSIA 1-1 UKRAINE	Moscow	EQ
716	**23/02/2000**	**ISRAEL 4-1 RUSSIA**	**Haifa**	**FR**

717	29/03/2000	ISRAEL	1-1	GEORGIA		Ashkelon	FR
718	26/04/2000	CZECH REP.	4-1	ISRAEL		Prague	FR
719	03/06/2000	GERMANY	3-2	CZECH REP.		Nuremburg	FR
720	07/06/2000	GERMANY	8-2	LIECHTENSTEIN		Freiburg	FR
721	12/06/2000	GERMANY	1-1	ROMANIA		Liege	EC
722	**17/06/2000**	**GERMANY**	**0-1**	**ENGLAND**		**Charleroi**	**EC**
723	20/06/2000	ENGLAND	2-3	ROMANIA		Charleroi	EC
724	24/06/2000	ROMANIA	0-2	ITALY		Brussels	EC
725	29/06/2000	NETHERL.	0-0	ITALY*	PEN	Amsterdam	EC
726	02/07/2000	ITALY	1-2	FRANCE	AET	Rotterdam	EC
727	02/09/2000	FRANCE	1-1	ENGLAND		St Denis	FR
728	04/10/2000	FRANCE	1-1	CAMEROON		St Denis	FR
729	07/10/2000	S. AFRICA	0-0	FRANCE		Johannesburg	FR
730	15/11/2000	TURKEY	0-4	FRANCE		Istanbul	FR
731	27/02/2001	FRANCE	1-0	GERMANY		St Denis	FR
732	24/03/2001	FRANCE	5-0	JAPAN		St Denis	FR
733	28/03/2001	SPAIN	2-1	FRANCE		Valencia	FR
734	25/04/2001	SPAIN	1-0	JAPAN		Cordoba	FR
735	02/06/2001	SPAIN	4-1	BOSNIA-HERZ.		Oviedo	WQ
736	06/06/2001	ISRAEL	1-1	SPAIN		Tel Aviv	WQ

737	01/09/2001	SPAIN	4-0	AUSTRIA	Valencia	WQ
738	05/09/2001	LIECHTENSTN	0-2	SPAIN	Vaduz	WQ
739	14/11/2001	SPAIN	1-0	MEXICO	Huelva	FR
740	13/02/2002	SPAIN	1-1	PORTUGAL	Barcelona	FR
741	27/03/2002	NETHERL.	1-0	SPAIN	Rotterdam	FR
742	17/05/2002	USA	0-2	NETHERL.	Foxboro	FR

THE 2002 WORLD CUP

UFWC champs the Netherlands failed to qualify for the 2002 FIFA World Cup Korea Japan™ (as it was officially known), representing something of a shock considering the nation's strong standing in world football. The Dutch finished behind Portugal and the Republic of Ireland in their qualifying group. Brazil won the official tournament in their absence.

743	21/08/2002	NORWAY	0-1	NETHERLANDS	Oslo	FR
744	07/09/2002	NETHERLANDS	3-0	BELARUS	Eindhoven	EQ
745	16/10/2002	AUSTRIA	0-3	NETHERLANDS	Vienna	EQ
746	20/11/2002	GERMANY	1-3	NETHERLANDS	G.kirchen	FR
747	12/02/2003	NETHERLANDS	1-0	ARGENTINA	Amsterdam	FR
748	29/03/2003	NETHERLANDS	1-1	CZECH REP.	Rotterdam	EQ
749	02/04/2003	MOLDOVA	1-2	NETHERLANDS	Tiraspol	EQ
750	30/04/2003	NETHERLANDS	1-1	PORTUGAL	Eindhoven	FR

751	07/06/2003	BELARUS 0-2 NETHERL.	Minsk	EQ
752	20/08/2003	BELGIUM 1-1 NETHERL.	Brussels	FR
753	06/09/2003	NETHERL. 3-1 AUSTRIA	Rotterdam	EQ
754	**10/09/2003**	**CZECH REP. 3-1 NETHERL.**	**Prague**	**EQ**
755	11/10/2003	AUSTRIA 2-3 CZECH REP.	Vienna	EQ
756	15/11/2003	CZECH REP. 5-1 CANADA	Teplice	FR
757	18/02/2004	ITALY 2-2 CZECH REP.	Palermo	FR
758	31/03/2004	REP. IRELAND 2-1 CZECH REP.	Dublin	FR
759	28/04/2004	POLAND 0-0 REP. IRELAND	Bydgoszcz	FR
760	27/05/2004	REP. IRELAND 1-0 ROMANIA	Dublin	FR
761	**29/05/2004**	**REP. IRELAND 0-3 NIGERIA**	**London**	**FR**
762	31/05/2004	NIGERIA 2-0 JAMAICA	London	FR
763	05/06/2004	NIGERIA 2-0 RWANDA	Abuja	WQ
764	20/06/2004	ANGOLA 1-0 NIGERIA	Luanda	WQ
765	03/07/2004	GABON 2-2 ANGOLA	Libreville	WQ
766	18/07/2004	ANGOLA* 1-1 BOTSWANA PEN	Luanda	CO
767	05/09/2004	ANGOLA 1-0 RWANDA	Luanda	WQ
768	19/09/2004	MOZAMBIQUE 0-1 ANGOLA	Maputo	CO
769	10/10/2004	ANGOLA 1-0 ZIMBABWE	Luanda	WQ
770	20/11/2004	ZAMBIA 0-0 ANGOLA* PEN	Lusaka	CO

THE COSAFA CUP

The COSAFA Cup, the championship of the Confederation of Southern African Football Associations, was initiated in 1997. The UFWC title has been contested at two consecutive COSAFA tournaments. First, in 2004, UFWC champs Angola won the COSAFA Cup. Then, in 2005, unofficial champs Zimbabwe did the UFWC / OSAFA double.

771	23/02/2005	CONGO	0-2	ANGOLA	Brazzaville	FR
772	**27/03/2005**	**ZIMBABWE**	**2-0**	**ANGOLA**	**Harare**	**WQ**
773	16/04/2005	ZIMBABWE	3-0	MOZAMBIQUE	Windhoek	CO
774	17/04/2005	ZIMBABWE	2-0	BOTSWANA	Windhoek	CO
775	05/06/2005	ZIMBABWE	1-0	GABON	Harare	WQ
776	19/06/2005	ALGERIA	2-2	ZIMBABWE	Oran	WQ
777	13/08/2005	ZIMBABWE	2-1	ANGOLA	Mmabatho	CO
778	14/08/2005	ZIMBABWE	1-0	ZAMBIA	Mmabatho	CO
779	28/08/2005	ZIMBABWE	0-0	MOZAMBIQUE	Harare	FR
780	04/09/2005	ZIMBABWE	3-1	RWANDA	Harare	WQ
781	08/10/2005	NIGERIA	5-1	ZIMBABWE	Abuja	WQ
782	16/11/2005	ROMANIA	3-0	NIGERIA	Bucharest	FR
783	26/02/2006	ARMENIA	0-2	ROMANIA	Nicosia	FR
784	01/03/2006	SLOVENIA	0-2	ROMANIA	Larnaca	FR

785	23/05/2006	URUGUAY 2-0 ROMANIA	Los Angeles	FR
786	27/05/2006	SERBIA & M. 1-1 URUGUAY	Belgrade	FR
787	30/05/2006	LIBYA 1-2 URUGUAY	Tunis	FR
788	02/06/2006	URUGUAY* 0-0 TUNISIA PEN	Tunis	FR

THE 2006 WORLD CUP

UFWC title holders Uruguay failed to qualify for the 2006 World Cup finals in Germany, finishing below Brazil, Argentina, Ecuador and Paraguay in their qualifying group, and then narrowly losing out on penalties in a play-off against Australia. Therefore the UFWC title was not contested at Germany 2006.

Further results and fixtures can be found at www.ufwc.co.uk.

OVERALL RANKINGS

At the time of publication, 43 nations have won the UFWC title. In the UFWC's all-time ranking system sides are awarded one ranking point for every title match victory. No points are awarded for a draw.

Scotland top the rankings table, having won more UFWC matches than any other nation. England are second, with the two British nations some way ahead of their opposition largely due to their dominance of the early game. The remainder of the top 10 is filled with football's usual suspects – the cream of international football in Argentina, Russia, the Netherlands, Brazil, Germany, Sweden, France, and Italy.

Further down the table, Wales are ranked 15th and Northern Ireland, who competed as Ireland until 1921, are ranked 31st. Australia, the Dutch Antilles, Israel, Mexico, and South Korea share 43rd place, having won one UFWC match each.

Scotland have won 11 more title matches than second-placed England, despite having played three fewer games. Overall, Scotland have won 59 percent of their UFWC clashes. In terms of percentage of games won, Sweden and Zimbabwe have the best records, having won 65 percent and 64 percent of their UFWC matches respectively.

A further 46 nations have played UFWC matches without ever winning. Of those sides, Finland and Norway have the worst records, having played 14 and 11 UFWC matches respectively without once being victorious.

In the table that follows, teams are ranked numerically by points won, then alphabetically. Point totals have been combined for sides that have officially played under different names and are recognised as doing so by FIFA, namely Germany and West Germany, Czech Republic and Czechoslovakia, Northern Ireland and Ireland, and Russia and the USSR.

RANK	TEAM	PLAYED	POINTS
1	SCOTLAND	145	85
2	ENGLAND	148	74
3	ARGENTINA	88	50
4	RUSSIA	67	41
5	NETHERLANDS	58	32
6	BRAZIL	62	29
7	GERMANY	61	27
8	SWEDEN	40	26
9	FRANCE	53	25
10	ITALY	52	24
11	CZECH REPUBLIC	40	15
11	SPAIN	28	15
13	HUNGARY	38	14
13	URUGUAY	45	14
15	AUSTRIA	35	12
15	WALES	73	12
17	CHILE	36	11
18	SWITZERLAND	34	9
19	COLOMBIA	25	8
19	ROMANIA	26	8
21	ANGOLA	14	7
21	PARAGUAY	26	7

21	PERU	26	7
21	ZIMBABWE	12	7
25	BULGARIA	22	6
26	BELGIUM	20	5
26	BOLIVIA	14	5
26	COSTA RICA	9	5
26	GREECE	18	5
26	NORTHERN IRELAND	63	5
26	YUGOSLAVIA	18	5
32	NIGERIA	7	4
32	POLAND	19	4
34	DENMARK	16	3
34	REPUBLIC OF IRELAND	10	3
36	ECUADOR	13	2
36	PORTUGAL	22	2
36	USA	8	2
39	AUSTRALIA	3	1
39	DUTCH ANTILLES	4	1
39	ISRAEL	8	1
39	MEXICO	20	1
39	S KOREA	2	1

UNDISPUTED CHAMPIONS

Seven nations have held both the official World Cup and unofficial UFWC title simultaneously, thus having claim to the title of Undisputed Football World Champions. Italy were the first side to achieve this feat, winning the World Cup in 1938, and winning the UFWC title in 1939. Italy, West Germany, Brazil, Argentina, and France have all been undisputed football world champions twice, and Uruguay and England have both had the honour once. The following table shows the undisputed champions in chronological order, and the number of games won by each side while in possession of the undisputed crown.

TEAM	DATE	GAMES
ITALY	04/06/1939	4
URUGUAY	28/03/1953	2
WEST GERMANY	08/06/1958	2
BRAZIL	19/06/1958	9
ENGLAND	30/07/1966	3
WEST GERMANY	07/07/1974	4
ARGENTINA	25/06/1978	4
ITALY	11/07/1982	1
ARGENTINA	29/06/1986	1
BRAZIL	29/03/1998	1
FRANCE	12/07/1998	6
FRANCE	02/07/2000	4

UFWC RULES

1. UFWC matches are played according to the official regulations of the governing body under which the game is played.

2. A UFWC title match is any FIFA accredited International 'A' match involving the current UFWC title-holder. According to FIFA: 'An International "A" match shall be a match that has been arranged between two National A Associations affiliated to the Federation and for which both Associations field their first national representative team.' This includes most friendly matches.

3. The winner of any such UFWC title match is declared the current UFWC title-holder.

4. UFWC rankings are calculated via a simple points system. Teams are awarded one ranking point for winning a UFWC title match, either as holder or challenger. No points are awarded for drawing a title match. If two or more teams have equal ranking points they share that rank, and are listed alphabetically in the ranking table.

5. In the result of a dispute, the decision of the UFWC is final.

HALL OF FAME

THE WEBSITE

Keep up to date with news, results, fixtures, match reports, statistics, features, and lots more at the official UFWC website:

www.ufwc.co.uk

If you have any questions or comments about the UFWC you can post them on the message board or email info@ufwc.co.uk.

THE AUTHOR

Paul Brown is the author of football books *Balls: Tales From Football's Nether Regions* (2005) and *Black & White Army* (2003), and true crime tale *The Rocketbelt Caper* (2005). He wrote about the Unofficial Football World Championships in the October 2004 issue of *FourFourTwo* magazine. He lives in Tyneside and supports Newcastle United and England.

READ MORE FROM TONTO PRESS

Dial M For Monkey

by Adam Maxwell

ISBN 0955218322, paperback, 124 pp, £7.99

Adam Maxwell's first collection of short stories is inventive, funny, dark, and hugely entertaining, ranging from a bizarre quest to find a dead rockstar's limb (Jim Morrison's Leg) to a memorable warning about the hidden dan-gers of building sites (the acclaimed Shooting Jelly With A Shotgun).

Tonto Short Stories

Edited by Paul Brown and Stuart Wheatman

ISBN 0955218306, paperback, 224 pp, £9.99

Tonto Press launches its search for new writing talent with an anthology of twenty fresh stories by twenty exciting writers. Eclectic, absorbing, affecting, and memorable, this page-turning collection represents the very best of short but sweet original fiction.

Wor Al

A Fans' Tribute To Alan Shearer

ISBN 0955218330, paperback, 192 pp, £6.99

A unique tribute to England hero and Geordie legend Alan Shearer, looking at his brilliant career through the eyes of fanzine, website and terrace writers.

Available from bookshops and www.tontopress.com

Printed in the United Kingdom
by Lightning Source UK Ltd.
111562UKS00001B/169-210